SHEPHERD'S NOTES

SHEPHERD'S NOTES

When you need a guide through the Scriptures

I & II *Samuel*

BROADMAN
&HOLMAN
PUBLISHERS

Nashville, Tennessee

Shepherd's Notes—*1 and 2 Samuel*
© 1998
by Broadman & Holman Publishers
Nashville, Tennessee
All rights reserved
Printed in the United States of America

0–8054–9063–9
Dewey Decimal Classification: 222.4
Subject Heading: BIBLE. O.T. SAMUEL
Library of Congress Card Catalog Number: 98–18014

Library of Congress Cataloging-in-Publication Data

First and Second Samuel/ Robert Bergen, editor
      p. cm.   — (Shepherd's notes)
    Includes bibliographical references.
    ISBN 0–8054–9063–9
    1. Bible. O.T. Samuel—Study and teaching.   I. Bergen, Robert. D. II. Series.
BS1325.5.F57   1998
222'.407—dc21

98–18014
CIP

1 2 3 4 5 6   03 02 01 00 99 98

CONTENTS

Dear Reader:

Shepherd's Notes are designed to give you a quick, step-by-step overview of every book of the Bible. They are not meant to be substitutes for the biblical text; rather, they are study guides intended to help you explore the wisdom of Scripture in personal or group study and to apply that wisdom successfully in your own life.

Shepherd's Notes guide you through the main themes of each book of the Bible and illuminate fascinating details through appropriate commentary and reference notes. Historical and cultural background information brings the Bible into sharper focus.

Six different icons, used throughout the series, call your attention to historical-cultural information, Old Testament and New Testament references, word pictures, unit summaries, and personal application for everyday life.

Whether you are a novice or a veteran at Bible study, I believe you will find *Shepherd's Notes* a resource that will take you to a new level in your mining and applying the riches of Scripture.

In Him,

David R. Shepherd
Editor-in-Chief

DESIGNED FOR THE BUSY USER

Shepherd's Notes for 1, 2 Samuel is designed to provide an easy-to-use tool for getting a quick handle on these significant Bible books, important features, and for gaining an understanding of their messages. Information available in more difficult-to-use reference works has been incorporated into the *Shepherd's Notes* format. This brings you the benefits of many advanced and expensive works packed into one small volume.

Shepherd's Notes are for laymen, pastors, teachers, small-group leaders and participants, as well as the classroom student. Enrich your personal study or quiet time. Shorten your class or small-group preparation time as you gain valuable insights into the truths of God's Word that you can pass along to your students or group members.

DESIGNED FOR QUICK ACCESS

Bible students with time constraints will especially appreciate the timesaving features built into the *Shepherd's Notes*. All features are intended to aid a quick and concise encounter with the heart of the messages of 1, 2 Samuel.

Concise Commentary. Short sections provide quick "snapshots" of the themes of these books, highlighting important points and other information.

Outlined Text. Comprehensive outlines cover the entire text of 1, 2 Samuel. This is a valuable feature for following each book's flow, allowing for a quick, easy way to locate a particular passage.

Shepherd's Notes. These summary statements or capsule thoughts appear at the close of every key section of the narratives. While functioning in part as a quick summary, they also deliver the essence of the message presented in the sections which they cover.

Icons. Various icons in the margin highlight recurring themes in the books of 1, 2 Samuel, aiding in selective searching or tracing of those themes.

Sidebars and Charts. These specially selected features provide additional background information to your study or preparation. Charts offer a quick overview of important subjects. Sidebars include definitions as well as cultural, historical, and biblical insights.

Questions to Guide Your Study. These thought-provoking questions and discussion starters are designed to encourage interaction with the truth and principles of God's Word.

DESIGNED TO WORK FOR YOU

Personal Study. Using the *Shepherd's Notes* with a passage of Scripture can enlighten your study and take it to a new level. At your fingertips is information that would require searching several volumes to find. In addition, many points of application occur throughout the volume, contributing to personal growth.

Teaching. Outlines frame the text of 1, 2 Samuel, providing a logical presentation of their messages. Capsule thoughts designated as "Shepherd's Notes" provide summary statements for presenting the essence of key points and events. Application icons point out personal application of the messages of the books. Historical Context icons indicate where cultural and historical background information is supplied.

Group Study. Shepherd's Notes can be an excellent companion volume to use for gaining a quick but accurate understanding of the messages of 1, 2 Samuel. Each group member can benefit from having his or her own copy. The *Note's* format accommodates the study of themes throughout 1, 2 Samuel. Leaders may use its flexible features to prepare for group sessions or use them during group sessions. Questions to guide your study can spark discussion of 1, 2 Samuel's key points and truths to be discovered in these delightful books.

LIST OF MARGIN ICONS USED IN 1, 2 SAMUEL

 Shepherd's Notes. Placed at the end of each section, a capsule statement provides the reader with the essence of the message of that section.

 Historical Context. To indicate historical information—historical, biographical, cultural—and provide insight on the understanding or interpretation of a passage.

 Old Testament Reference. Used when the writer refers to Old Testament passages or when Old Testament passages illuminate a text.

 New Testament Reference. Used when the writer refers to New Testament passages that are either fulfilled prophecy, an antitype of an Old Testament type, or a New Testament text which in some other way illuminates the passages under discussion.

 Personal Application. Used when the text provides a personal or universal application of truth.

 Word Picture. Indicates that the meaning of a specific word or phrase is illustrated so as to shed light on it.

INTRODUCTION

Book of Jashar (Upright)

This book, quoted twice in the Old Testament, probably consisted of poems on important events in Israel's history collected during the time of David or Solomon.

AUTHOR AND DATE OF WRITING

Substantially the work of the prophet Samuel, 1 and 2 Samuel were written in the eleventh century B.C. However, their obvious connectedness with 1, 2 Kings, as well as literary clues in the text (e.g., mention of the length of David's reign [2 Sam. 5:4], use of the phrase *"the kings of Judah"* [1 Sam. 27:6], indication that a term used as late as the eighth century B.C. was out-of-date at the time of writing [1 Sam. 9:9]), indicate that these books reached their final form during the Babylonian Exile or shortly thereafter and were written using at least one other written source (the Book of Jashar, see 2 Sam. 1:18).

AUDIENCE

The first readers of the finished form of 1, 2 Samuel were Jews living in either the sixth or fifth centuries B.C. They were concerned about putting their nation back together again following the destruction of Jerusalem by Babylon. They were also interested in tracing out the historical roots of theological and political issues that affected their lives.

FUNCTIONS AND PURPOSES

The books of 1, 2 Samuel were written to serve many different functions. First and most importantly, they were intended to be used in the Jewish religious community as Holy Scripture, that is, as the completely authoritative and trustworthy Word of God, providing guidance and encouragement to their hearers. As Scripture they reinforce the teachings of the Torah by providing historical examples of both obedience and disobedience to God's Law. At the same time they lay a solid foundation for understanding the life and ministry of Jesus Christ, the ultimate son of David.

They also function as history. In this regard they describe Israel's transition to a monarchical form of government and provide information about Israel's last two judges and first two kings. These events took place over an indeterminate period of time stretching across parts of three centuries from the late twelfth century B.C. to the early tenth century B.C. These books also supply details about the religious history of Israel, including information about significant worship centers, priestly leaders, and the sacred ark of the covenant.

The Hebrew Bible consists of four major sections: the Law ("Torah"), the Former Prophets and Latter Prophets, and the Writings. While Jews accept all of these parts as the Word of God, the Torah is treated with special reverence. Within the Hebrew Bible, the Prophets and the Writings function to confirm, clarify, and celebrate the message of the Torah.

Another purpose for writing 1, 2 Samuel was to defend certain leading figures in the Israelite monarchy against charges made against them. Three controversial situations arose during David's lifetime, and each of them needed an accounting. The issues were (1) displacement of Saul's family line by David's on the throne of Israel, (2) Solomon's rise to kingship even though he wasn't next in line to become king, and (3) the Abiatharites' loss of their role as leaders in Israelite worship. The books provide a justification for each of these outcomes in Israelite history.

Another important purpose of 1, 2 Samuel was to reinforce theological truths found throughout the Torah. For further discussion of this point, see the Theology section below.

STRUCTURE AND CONTENT

The narratives found in 1, 2 Samuel center on three persons: Samuel (1 Sam. 1–7), Saul (1 Sam. 8–14), and David (1 Sam. 15–2 Sam.

20). Materials in these narrative sections are normally presented in chronological order.

An appendix at the end of these books (2 Sam. 21–24) provides materials that illustrate David's roles in his relationship with God. Materials found in the appendix are in the form of narrative, lists, and poetry related to David's life. They are taken from various points in David's life and are, therefore, not part of the chronological scheme of the earlier portions of the books.

LITERARY STYLE AND TEXTUAL ISSUES

Originally composed in the Hebrew language using a classic narrative style, 1, 2 Samuel richly draw portraits of the three leading characters. These books are among the most detailed in the Old Testament. In fact, David is the subject of more narrative verbs than any other character in the Old Testament—even more than Moses.

The Hebrew manuscripts of 1, 2 Samuel are considered by many scholars to be among the most defective in the Old Testament.

Comparisons between the Masoretic text and those of the Septuagint and Dead Sea Scrolls reveal many, mostly minor discrepancies. An example is found in 1 Samuel 11:1, where a short paragraph containing additional background material is absent in the Masoretic text but present in other ancient textual witnesses. (To see the material in question, consult the New Revised Standard Version.)

THEOLOGY

Like other portions of the Former Prophets, Latter Prophets, and Writings (three of the four divisions of the Hebrew Bible), 1, 2 Samuel were not written to inject new theological truths into Israelite society. Instead, they were carefully

Texts of the Old Testament

The Masoretic text is the primary Hebrew language text. The Septuagint is a Greek translation of the Old Testament. The Dead Sea Scrolls are early Hebrew manuscripts.

Many contemporary Old Testament scholars believe that the books of Deuteronomy, Joshua, Judges, 1 Samuel, 2 Samuel, 1 Kings, and 2 Kings were the work of an anonymous individual or group of individuals known as the Deuteronomist/ Deuteronomistic Historians. Scholars who hold this view note that these books emphasize common themes: the need to reject idols and worship only the Lord, God's unique selection of Israel to be His people, God's gift of a homeland for Israel, the need for obedience to the Torah, the need for one central place of worship, and the proper roles of prophets and kings.

The life of Hannah demonstrates the tremendous potential for a godly, loving mother to change the world through a child conceived in faith and dedicated to the Lord.

The life of David inspires us to take great risks in confronting "giants" that hinder us and our society, confident that God is able to help us achieve undreamed of victories. David's life also reminds us that sexual misconduct, even if limited to a single act, may bring devastating consequences into our lives. At the same time, it also shows us that God stands ready to forgive even the darkest sins we might commit when we confess our sins to Him.

written to reiterate, reinforce, and clarify the theological truths of the Torah (the first five books of the Old Testament). Especially important in these books are the concepts of (1) the need for wholehearted obedience to God, (2) God's establishment of a covenant for the benefit of His people (in this case, covenantal provision of leadership for Israel through the family line of David), (3) the presence of God among His people (especially as it is connected with the ark of the covenant, and as God was with David), and (4) the relationship that exists between possession of the land of Israel and the people's obedience to God (when Israel sinned, enemies took control of portions of Israel; also David himself was forced to leave Israel for a time as a consequence of his sin with Bathsheba).

THE MEANING OF 1, 2 SAMUEL FOR TODAY

The books of 1, 2 Samuel encourage and instruct us to live lives of wholehearted obedience to God (see 1 Sam. 15:22). Through the examples of Hannah and David, they teach us that God can use both women and men, who may be unappreciated or rejected by others, to do great things for Him—if they possess great faith in Him.

- - - - - - - - - - - - - -

THE LORD REWARDS HANNAH'S FAITH (1:1–2:11)

Elkanah's Wives (1:1–2)

Elkanah, a pious Levite residing in Ramathaim-zophim in the rural regions of Ephraim, had two wives, Hannah and Peninnah. Elkanah's bigamy was probably motivated by the fact that his beloved wife Hannah was unable to produce an heir for him, a matter of vital concern in that society. But the bigamous relationship produced great hardship for Hannah, who was harassed by Peninnah, the fertile rival wife.

Family Worship (1:3–8)

Each year Elkanah would take his family to Shiloh, Israel's central worship site and the one that housed the ark of the covenant, Israel's most sacred object. A climactic part of the family pilgrimage was a feast that included meat, a rarity in the typical Israelite diet. Each wife was given a portion of meat that corresponded to the number of children to which she had given birth. Thus for Hannah, this otherwise joyous occasion was a time of great frustration and anxiety because it served as a reminder that the Lord had closed her womb.

Hannah's Sorrow (1:9–18)

One year Hannah became so upset during the annual meal that she left the family celebration in order to weep and pray alone in the worship center. There she made a vow to God, promising that the first child that He allowed her to bear would be made a lifelong Nazirite, a special servant to the Lord. Her emotionally charged, tearful prayer caught the attention of Eli, the

According to 1 Chronicles 6:21–22, Elkanah was a member of the Kohathite clan of the tribe of Levi. Since Levites were not given any connected tribal territory of their own, they lived in cities scattered throughout the rest of the land of Israel (see Num. 35:2–5; Josh. 21:3–42). Kohathites were given four cities in Ephraim (see Josh. 21:20–22), but they apparently were allowed to live in other villages there as well, including Ramathaim.

elderly high priest of the Shiloh sanctuary, who mistakenly accused Hannah of being a disorderly drunk. Hannah meekly explained to the priest that she was actually pleading with God for an end to her infertility. When Eli understood this, he asked God to answer her request. Hannah then rejoined her family, full of peace and hope.

Answered Prayer (1:19–20)

Soon after the family's return to their home in Ramah, God answered Hannah's prayer, and she conceived a child. The child born to her was a boy whom she named Samuel, a name expressing the fact that she had asked the Lord for him.

Baby Samuel (1:21–28)

Until the child was weaned, probably a period of three to five years, Hannah devoted herself to nurturing the child in the home. After that time, Hannah and Elkanah brought Samuel to Shiloh, to make him a servant assisting Eli in maintaining the worship site. The parents' presentation was accompanied by a lavish gift of sacrificial animals and agricultural products and was concluded with a time of worship.

Hannah's humiliating hardship actually played a useful role in her life. It drove her to God and forced her to look to Him for her hope and help. In the end her faith was mightily rewarded. The birth of her son Samuel not only ended her disgrace but also brought onto the stage of history Israel's greatest judge and first kingmaker.

Hannah's Presentation of Samuel (2:1–11)

At the time of Hannah's presentation of Samuel to Eli, Hannah reacted not by crying but by uttering a jubilant prayer, in fact the longest prayer by a woman recorded in the Bible. Hannah's highly

Hannah's inability to bear a child for her husband links her story with those of other women who played a major role in the history of Israel. The wives of three of the most important men in the early history of Israel—Sarah (wife of Abraham), Rebekah (wife of Isaac), and Rachel (wife of Jacob)—were also unable for a time in their married lives to bear children. However, in each case God ultimately gave them sons that played a significant role in Israel's history.

theological prayer affirms that God has blessed her and answered her prayer. As she noted, the Lord is the great reverser of fortunes. He can make the weak strong, the hungry full, the poor wealthy, the humiliated honored, and the barren woman fertile. He also possesses the power to bring death and life and is the One who alone provides the resources for success in life. Prophetically, Hannah also confessed in her prayer that the Lord would give strength to His king, even though Israel had not yet had a king and would not have one until her son anointed one.

Following that prayer, Elkanah and Hannah returned to Ramathaim-zophim, leaving their son at Shiloh in Eli's care.

- By her faith in God, Elkanah's barren Hannah overcame the curse of childlessness and gave birth to Samuel. By her faithful commitment to motherhood, Hannah lovingly nurtured Samuel during his early years, preparing him for a lifetime of society-changing service to the Lord.

QUESTIONS TO GUIDE YOUR STUDY

1. Who were Samuel's parents?
2. What was unusual about Samuel's birth?
3. How did Hannah express her gratitude to God for her first son?
4. What is the major theme of Hannah's song?

THE LORD BLESSES HANNAH'S FAMILY BUT JUDGES ELI'S FAMILY (2:12–36)

Eli's Sons (vv. 12–17)

Eli had two sons, Hophni and Phinehas. Since Eli was too old to serve as an officiating priest, the task fell to Hophni and Phinehas. However, these men were morally corrupt and conducted themselves unworthily in fulfilling their duties. This was evidenced in two ways—by the improper way they handled the animal sacrifices and the way they abused the women who served voluntarily in maintaining the worship center. Instead of setting aside God's portion of a sacrifice first, as the Torah required, they took theirs first; and when they did, they took parts of the animal that priests were not permitted to have. Though both men were married, they forced the female volunteers at Shiloh to have intimate relations with them. These abuses by God's earthly representatives displeased the Lord.

Faithful Servant (2:18–36)

Unlike Eli's sons, Elkanah's son Samuel faithfully served the Lord. Samuel received support from his mother in his efforts, who brought him new clothing each year to use in his work at Shiloh. Eli pronounced a blessing on Elkanah and Hannah during their annual visits, and indeed, God's blessing was upon them. Over the years Hannah gave birth to three additional sons and two daughters.

Eli's family, by contrast, was under God's curse. Though Eli warned his sons against continuing in their sinful ways, they ignored him. As a result, God determined to kill them for their unrepentant, sinful ways. Eli, too, was under God's judgment for failing to restrain his sons and for participating in their sins by eating the sacrificial portions they had wrongly taken from their fellow Israelites. God's stern judgment, announced by an unnamed prophet, was that Eli's family line would be disqualified from the priesthood, and its male members would suffer premature and often violent death.

- Hannah's faith overflowed in praise, and
- God rewarded her faith with five additional
- children. Her young son Samuel, meanwhile,
- faithfully served the Lord at Shiloh. Eli's
- sons, by contrast, angered the Lord through
- their selfish and sinful service. This resulted
- in a harsh prophetic judgment against Eli's
- family that promised an end to that family's
- domination of Israel's priestly activities.

The family lines of Eli and Elkanah present a vivid picture of the contrast between the blessings and curses of God mentioned in the Law of Moses (see Lev. 26, Deut. 28). Elkanah and Hannah put God first in their lives, and God rewarded them with a multiplication of life within their family. On the other hand, Eli's family members put themselves ahead of God and their duties to Him. As a result, they experienced God's curse. They permanently lost their privileged position in society (see 1 Kings 2:26–27, 35), and experienced violence and death as well. Ultimately, another priestly line, the Zadokites, was given the duties once assigned to Eli's family line.

QUESTIONS TO GUIDE YOUR STUDY

1. Why was God not pleased with Eli's sons?
2. What were the consequences of God's displeasure with Eli's family?

1 SAMUEL 3

THE LORD MAKES SAMUEL ISRAEL'S PROPHET (3:1–21)

Samuel's Call (vv. 1–8)

Part of Samuel's service at Shiloh involved spending the night in the sanctuary in order to keep the sacred lamp burning till dawn. While sleeping near the ark of the covenant, the boy heard someone call his name. Assuming it was Eli, he asked the elderly priest what he wanted. Eli told Samuel that it was not he who had summoned the boy and told him to return to bed. When Samuel arose twice more that same night to ask Eli when he thought he heard someone call him, Eli told him it was the Lord speaking to him and instructed the boy to ask the Lord to speak further with him.

According to the Torah, Eli was not allowed to serve actively in the temple because he was more than fifty years old (see Num. 4:46–47; 1 Sam. 4:15). This was apparently why Samuel was given the responsibility of keeping the lamp burning in the sanctuary (Exod. 27:20).

Prophetic Message (vv. 9–21)

Samuel obeyed; and when the voice spoke to him the fourth time in the sanctuary that night, the Lord gave the lad a prophetic message that confirmed the harsh prophecies previously announced against Eli and his family line. Though understandably hesitant to tell Eli what he had heard from the Lord, Samuel did so when Eli ordered him to.

This prophetic word revealed to young Samuel proved to be the first in a long line of revelations that came throughout his entire lifetime. The Lord was with Samuel, and his reputation as an accurate and insightful prophet soon made him famous among all the tribes of Israel. People made treks to Shiloh to receive a word from God through the young prophet.

- *Samuel grew from a naive child to the most*
- *insightful prophet in Israel since the days of*
- *Moses. Unable to recognize the word of the*
- *Lord at first, the boy was taught by Eli how*
- *to respond to the Lord's call. With Eli's help,*
- *Samuel also learned that he must boldly and*
- *fully declare the prophetic word from God to*
- *those to whom it is directed.*

QUESTIONS TO GUIDE YOUR STUDY

1. Describe Samuel's first experience of hearing God's voice.
2. How did Samuel respond to what God told him?

ELI'S FAMILY IS DEVASTATED AND THE ARK OF GOD IS CAPTURED (4:1–22)

Philistine Battle (vv. 1–11)

About this time, the Israelites went to do battle with the Philistines.

The Philistine forces camped at Aphek, a city in Israelite territory, while the Israelite forces camped two miles away at Ebenezer. In the first encounter between these armies, Israel was soundly defeated; four thousand of their soldiers were killed. To avoid a repeat of this tragedy, the Israelites tried a new approach; they would be led into battle by their God. They accomplished this by having Eli's two sons carry the Lord's throne, the ark of the covenant, into battle. This tactic had proved successful earlier in Israel's history (see Josh 6:6–21). However, it failed miserably here. Though the Philistines were initially frightened by the presence of the ark among the Israelites, they fought all the harder in battle and routed the Israelites. In all they killed thirty thousand of their enemy, including Eli's two sons Hophni and Phinehas. In addition they captured the ark of the covenant, which they treated as a treasure, placing it in the temple of their god Dagon in the city of Ashdod.

Israelite Defeat (vv. 12–22)

News of the defeat reached the city of Shiloh, and the city mourned greatly. When the elderly priest Eli learned that the ark of the covenant had been captured by the Philistines and that his two sons were dead, he fell off a chair, causing him to break his neck and die. Phinehas's

The Philistines were a non-Semitic people who had come from other parts of the Mediterranean world to settle in the Promised Land in large numbers during the days of the Judges (see "Philistines," in *Holman Bible Dictionary*). They posed the single greatest military threat to Israel at that time.

Archaeological excavations conducted at the site of biblical Shiloh indicate that it was destroyed by fire in the mid-eleventh century B.C. Biblical evidence outside of 1 Samuel also suggests that the Philistines may have ransacked the city at this time (see Ps. 78:60; Jer. 7:12–14; 26:6, 9).

Shepherd's Notes, 1 Samuel 5

The ark of the covenant was considered to be Israel's holiest and most prized object. No wonder; it was God's throne (see 1 Sam. 4:4; see Exod. 25:20–22; Num. 7:89). God had commanded Moses to have the Israelites build the special object while they were encamped at Mount Sinai during their Exodus from Egypt. The ark consisted of a wooden box overlaid with gold. A specially constructed lid featured two carved cherubs. Inside the ark were kept the Ten Commandments (see Exod. 25:16; 40:20).

So sacred was the ark of the covenant that members of only one family—descendants of Aaron, Israel's first high priest—were ever permitted to view it (see Num. 4:4–6, 20). It was normally kept hidden from view in the Holy of Holies, the innermost room of Israel's worship center. The ark of the covenant disappeared from history at the time of the Babylonian Exile.

pregnant wife was so upset by the news that she went into premature labor and died during the birthing process. Just before dying, she named the son that was born Ichabod—"No Glory"—because of Israel's loss of the ark of the covenant.

1 SAMUEL 5

THE ARK OF THE COVENANT OPPRESSES THE PHILISTINES (5:1–12)

The Ark in Ashdod (vv. 1–5)

Though the Philistines placed the ark of the covenant in an inferior position before the statue of their god Dagon in Ashdod, they soon learned that Israel's God was actually the superior deity. When Dagon's priests opened up the temple the morning after placing the ark inside, they were shocked to discover that Dagon's image was lying face down on the ground in a position of worship before the ark. They quickly returned their god to his place, but it did not stay there long. The next morning Dagon was again on the ground, but this time it was shattered with the head and all limbs broken off.

Philistine Destruction (vv. 6–12)

The destruction of the Philistines' god was paralleled by the destruction of the Philistines themselves. A devastating plague broke out among the population in Ashdod that caused tumors to grow in the anal region of the peoples' bodies. The Philistines understood that Israel's God had brought this upon them, so they decided to get the ark out of their city before more damage was done. Accordingly, the ark was sent to the neighboring Philistine city of Gath, where the plague broke out anew. To protect themselves, the residents of Gath then moved the ark to Ekron, a third major Philistine city.

When the ark was being moved to Ekron, the people of that city panicked. They demanded that the ark be sent back to the Israelites instead. Before that could be done, however, many Philistines died in a divinely sent plague.

1 SAMUEL 6

THE ARK IS RETURNED TO ISRAEL (6:1–7:1)

The Ark Returned (6:1–6)
Israel's ark of the covenant remained in Philistine hands seven months. However the Philistines realized that keeping it any longer would only mean bringing more ruin on themselves, so they decided to return the ark to Israel. But they had to be careful how they returned the glorious throne of Israel's God, or they might suffer even more awful consequences. After consulting pagan priests and diviners, the Philistines decided to send an expensive guilt offering along to satisfy the offended deity: the offering consisted of five golden images of anal tumors and five golden rat statues—items actually considered detestable to the Lord!

A Test for the Ark (6:7–11)
Some Philistines doubted that their possession of the ark of God had actually been responsible for the recent plagues. So in order to prove the connection, a test was set up: The ark would be placed on a new cart and pulled by two cows that had calved but had never been yoked. If the untrained cows could resist their maternal instincts by walking past their bleating calves

In the biblical world, people believed that battles between two human armies were always accompanied by a heavenly battle between the armies' deities. For that reason, wars in the ancient Near East always had a religious dimension. Idols or symbols of the deities were often brought onto the battlefield to provide assurance of divine help. Strange weather occurrences during a battle were taken as proof of military movements of the gods and could be a reason for human armies to advance or retreat from the earthly conflict (see 1 Sam. 7:10; 2 Sam. 5:24). Soldiers in ancient Israel were accompanied by a priest and were expected to follow guidelines revealed to Moses at Mount Sinai (see Deut. 20). Failure of the soldiers to obey God's rules could result in God's bringing defeat on Israel's army (see Josh. 7).

God is holy and demands reverent respect. Though people who do not claim to follow Him, like the Philistines, might be expected to offend Him, God's people must be careful not to do things that would show disrespect toward the Lord and His commands. The Israelites of Beth Shemesh learned this lesson the hard way. During their time of celebration and sacrifice to God, they broke one of the most basic commands of their religion: They showed disrespect for the Lord by touching His earthly throne and peering inside the ark of the covenant. No earthly king would have permitted unauthorized persons to casually touch his throne—how much more so God! This thoughtless disrespect for God cost many Beth Shemeshites their lives.

What are we doing today in our own lives that reduces respect for God in our world? What can we do to show our love and reverent respect for Him?

and without any training could smoothly pull together in the yoke to keep the cart going straight down the road to Israel, then Israel's God had indeed caused the plagues.

The Ark Returned (6:12–7:1)

When the cart and cows were released, they went straight down the road to Israel, bringing the ark to the fields just outside of Beth Shemesh, a city inhabited by members of the priestly tribe of Levi. In celebration the surprised Beth Shemeshites offered God a sacrifice by chopping up and burning the cart and cows. Then, surprisingly, the Beth Shemeshites violated the Law of Moses by looking into the ark (see Num. 4:15). God judged the transgressors by killing 50,070 (the NIV, following another ancient version, says 70) of them. Not surprisingly, the Beth Shemeshites feared the ark and had it sent to the nearby Israelite village of Kiriath Jearim.

1 SAMUEL 7

GOD AND SAMUEL ROUT THE PHILISTINES (7:2–17)

Revival in Israel (vv. 2–12)

Some twenty years after the ark of the covenant was sent to Kiriath Jearim, the Israelites had a national revival and earnestly sought the Lord. Samuel headed the movement, leading the people to get rid of their idols and worship only the one true God.

After the people obeyed Samuel in this matter, he gathered the nation together in Mizpah for a meeting in which the people fasted and confessed their sins. The Philistines learned of the meeting, became concerned, and gathered their forces to attack Israel at Mizpah. The Israelites were frightened when they saw the Philistines advance against them, but Samuel offered a sacrifice and prayed to God for them. God responded with a miracle, causing the Philistine army to panic and run at the sound of thunder—a sound which the soldiers interpreted as the advance of an angry deity against them. The Israelites seized the opportunity, pursuing the fleeing army and killing all the stragglers. To commemorate the divinely sent victory, Samuel erected a stone monument which he named Ebenezer, "The Stone of Help."

Samuel's Influence (vv. 13–17)

As long as Samuel was alive, God helped Israel defeat the Philistines and establish a peaceful coexistence with the Amorites. All the Israelite towns from Ekron to Gath that had previously been conquered by the Philistines were returned to Israel. Samuel himself continued to provide leadership throughout central Israel by regularly holding court at four different sites in central Israel: Bethel, Gilgal, Mizpah, and his hometown of Ramah.

Samuel created a visible testimony to God's saving work in the life of Israel. During times of doubt or discouragement Israel could look at that rock and remember God's character and power. What reminders of God's saving work have you put into your home to encourage you during times of trouble and doubt?

■ *Under Samuel's leadership Israel experi-*
■ *enced national revival. Victory over their*
■ *enemies, the Philistines, accompanied their*
■ *return to God. The Israelites continued to*
■ *experience victory against the Philistines as*
■ *long as Samuel was their leader. Samuel*
■ *exercised his capable administration*
■ *throughout central Israel by regularly trav-*
■ *eling to four different locations where people*
■ *could seek justice.*

15

QUESTIONS TO GUIDE YOUR STUDY

1. What happened when the Philistines captured the ark of the covenant?
2. What happened at Mizpah, and what is the significance of that event?

1 SAMUEL 8

ISRAEL SEEKS A KING (8:1–22)

Desire for a King (vv. 1–5)

A major shift in Israelite governance occurred when Samuel grew old and tried to install his sons Joel and Abijah as his successors. Because Joel and Abijah were unjust judges who took bribes, the leaders of Israel's tribes rejected them and demanded a king "such as all the other nations have" (v. 5, NIV) to rule over the nation.

Samuel's Displeasure (vv. 16–18)

This request displeased Samuel, who understood the people's demand for a king to be a rejection of God's leadership. In the Law of Moses the Lord was called a king. When Samuel prayed about the situation, God told the prophet to honor the people's request but also to warn them of the consequences associated with their choice. Samuel cautioned them that kings would take much from them: their children to serve in the palace and army and a portion of their grain, grapes, olives, and animals. Kings would make the Israelites virtual slaves.

Samuel's Acceptance of Israel's Wishes (vv. 19–22)

Knowing all this, the people of Israel still demanded a king. They wanted a king because they believed a king who maintained a standing army was the only way to be assured of protection against foreign armies. When Samuel heard the people repeat their desire for a king, he accepted their request but told them to return to their homes until God had made known His choice for the one who would become Israel's first king. That choice would be revealed soon.

■ *Israel's elders made an epoch-changing*
■ *request of Samuel when they asked for a king*
■ *to rule over them. The request spelled an end*
■ *to rule by judges and amounted to a rejection*
■ *of God as Israel's king. In spite of the latter,*
■ *God agreed to their request and directed*
■ *Samuel to do the same.*

1 SAMUEL 9–10

GOD CHOOSES SAUL TO BE ISRAEL'S FIRST KING (9:1–10:16)

Saul, Son of Kish (9:1–14)

Saul was the son of a Benjamite named Kish, who lived in Gibeah, a wealthy man who owned slaves, donkeys, and oxen. When Kish's donkeys escaped one day, Saul was sent out with a slave to retrieve them. After an extensive but unsuccessful search of the region, Saul and the slave paid a visit to the elderly prophet/judge Samuel to seek his help in their task.

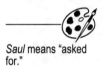

Saul means "asked for."

God's Choice for Israel's King (9:15–20)

In advance of Saul's visit, God had informed Samuel that Saul was coming and that the young man was God's choice to become Israel's first king. When Saul came to Samuel, the prophet immediately brought him to a special

All buildings had flat roofs in the ancient Near East. The roof of Israelite houses often functioned as a sort of terrace on which people might walk during the daytime (see 2 Sam. 11:2; 16:22) and sleep at night during the warmer seasons of the year.

Anointing was a practice carried out by priests and prophets of the Lord in the Old Testament. The priest or prophet would pour out a small amount of sacred, spiced olive oil on the top of the head of an individual selected by God's prophet to serve as a priest or king. The act symbolized the power and presence of God's coming upon an individual to enable the person to do the Lord's work.

sacrificial meal—perhaps a new moon festival, where he was made the guest of honor. Samuel also told Saul that the donkeys had safely returned home and that Saul was soon to become Israel's most honored citizen, i.e., king of the land.

Saul's Anointing (9:21–10:16)

Saul attended the special meal and then spent the night in Ramah as a guest of the prophet Samuel. Before Saul left the city the next morning, Samuel privately poured a flask of olive oil on Saul's head, signifying Saul's divine selection and special empowerment for the office of king. This significant, symbolic act was accompanied by predictions regarding certain events that would occur between the time Saul left Samuel and the time he arrived home, the most important one being that God's Spirit would come upon Saul and that he would prophesy. The predicted events all occurred, thereby confirming that Saul was God's choice to become Israel's first king and at the same time empowering him for the task. Though Saul now knew of God's plans for him, he did not tell any of his family members at this time.

■ *God chose Saul, the son of a wealthy Ben-*
■ *jamite named Kish, to be Israel's first king.*
■ *When Saul was sent out to look for the fam-*
■ *ily's lost donkeys, he met the prophet Sam-*
■ *uel, who privately marked him for his new*
■ *role by anointing him. Shortly thereafter, the*
■ *Holy Spirit came upon Saul.*

SAUL IS PUBLICLY INSTALLED AS ISRAEL'S FIRST KING (10:17–27)

A Religious Convocation (vv. 17–19)

Samuel summoned the Israelites together for a religious convocation at Mizpah, a city in the tribal territory of Benjamin. The process of publicly identifying the king was carried out by first selecting a tribe from which God's choice would come. The tribe of Benjamin was chosen. After that the specific Benjamite clan was chosen, and then from that clan the individual was set apart. In this manner Saul was chosen and given formal recognition as Israel's divinely selected monarch.

Rules for the King (vv. 20–25)

An awkward moment arose in the process when Saul failed to appear before the group after having been singled out. He was eventually found hiding among the supplies at the edge of the camp.

When Saul finally appeared before his fellow Israelites, he was warmly received—in part because he looked like a king, being a head taller than any other Israelite. Before dismissing the assembly, Samuel explained to the group God's rules related to kingship. The prophet then made a written copy of these rules, which were deposited alongside other sacred materials before the Lord.

Saul's Return Home (vv. 26–27)

Since there was no capital city or royal palace at that time, Saul returned to his hometown of Gibeah. He was accompanied by some valiant men who would become the core of Israel's standing army. Many people brought Saul gifts to celebrate his inauguration, though not all did. Some troublemakers heckled him and

Saul's height impressed the Israelites, because it made him look more impressive. But at the same time, it identified him with the "other nations," that is, people outside the covenant: the Canaanites (Num. 13:32–33), Anakites (Deut. 2:10), a Philistine (1 Sam. 17:4), an Egyptian (1 Chron. 11:23), Sabeans (Isa. 45:14), and an Amorite (Amos 2:9) were all considered tall. No other Israelite in the Bible besides Saul is referred to as "tall."

expressed their doubts about his ability to provide effective leadership.

■ *At a large public meeting held in the Ben-*
■ *jamite city of Mizpah, a gathering involving*
■ *all Israel, Saul was formally selected as*
■ *Israel's first king. Samuel used the occasion*
■ *to explain God's rules for kingship. Most of*
■ *the citizens rejoiced at Saul's selection,*
■ *though some despised him. Following the*
■ *meeting, Saul returned to his home in*
■ *Gibeah, since there was no royal city or*
■ *palace in Israel at that time.*

QUESTIONS TO GUIDE YOUR STUDY

1. What was Israel's primary reason for wanting a king?

2. How did Samuel know that Saul was to be the first king?

1 SAMUEL 11

SAUL DEFEATS THE AMMONITES AND RESCUES JABESH GILEAD (11:1–15)

Ammon's Siege of Jabesh Gilead (vv. 1–5)

Years before Saul's time, women from Jabesh Gilead were forced to marry Benjamite men in order to repopulate the tribe of Benjamin (see Judg. 21:14). Therefore, it was natural for them to ask Benjamin for help in their time of trouble. Saul may even have been a descendant of the Jabesh Gileadites.

After Saul was publicly anointed as king, Nahash, the king of Ammon, laid siege to the Israelite city of Jabesh Gilead, located east of the Jordan in the tribal territory of Manasseh. Nahash threatened to gouge out the right eye of every person in the city if they did not voluntarily submit to him. Before surrendering to the Ammonites, the Jabesh Gileadites sent a desperate plea to Saul, asking the new king to come to their rescue.

Victory over the Ammonites (vv. 6–15)

The Spirit of God came upon Saul when he heard the Jabesh Gileadites' request, and he boldly took the lead in amassing an all-Israelite army to come to the aid of the oppressed city. Saul led the troops brilliantly, splitting them into three groups around the enemy camp and then attacking the unsuspecting Ammonites just before dawn. The Ammonite army suffered a crushing defeat, and the city of Jabesh Gilead was saved.

Following the victory Samuel, Saul, and the rest of the Israelites went to the Benjamite city of Gilgal. There a great religious celebration was held and Saul's kingship was reaffirmed.

The Spirit of God came upon other Old Testament figures to enable them to do battle with enemies of Israel. Among them were Othniel (Judg. 3:10), Jephthah (Judg. 11:29), and Samson (Judg. 14:6; 15:14).

■ *As Israel's new king, Saul was called upon to*
■ *lead the nation against the Ammonites, who*
■ *were threatening the Israelite city of Jabesh*
■ *Gilead. Saul successfully amassed a large*
■ *volunteer army and led Israel to an impres-*
■ *sive victory. In celebration Samuel, Saul, and*
■ *all Israel went to Gilgal to offer sacrifices to*
■ *God and reaffirm Saul's kingship.*

1 SAMUEL 12 ················

SAMUEL DELIVERS HIS FINAL WORDS TO ALL ISRAEL (12:1–25)

Samuel's Last Address (vv. 1–5)

Samuel used the public assembly at Gilgal as an occasion to address all Israel for the last time in his life. The speech was a serious one. First, the elderly prophet/judge asked those he had served to evaluate his conduct as judge. The people commended him by noting that neither had he stolen, cheated, or oppressed any of them, nor had he ever taken a bribe.

Israel's Sin (vv. 6–18)

Samuel met with the Israelites during the time of the wheat harvest—sometime during late May or early June. Israel had two rainy seasons, known as the early rains (Heb. *yoreh*), beginning in late October; and the latter rains (Heb. *malqosh*), beginning in March and extending until early May. In most years, rains never occurred outside of these times.

Following that, Samuel then evaluated the people of Israel's behavior in their relationship with God. He noted that fear of an earthly king—Nahash of the Ammonites—had caused the Israelites to turn away from their heavenly King and seek an earthly king to lead them. This lack of trust in their ultimate King was a sin. Proof of God's displeasure came in the form of a freakish and unwelcome rainstorm that boiled up as Samuel spoke; because of the time of year that it came, the rain threatened the ripe wheat crop.

Israel Seeks Forgiveness (vv. 19–25)

After the storm, Samuel assured the frightened assembly that God would forgive them of their sin. However, the Israelites would have to be careful to obey all of the Lord's commands to avoid offending Him further. Samuel concluded his final address to Israel with two statements: first, an assurance that he would continue to pray for them; and second, a warning that if they continued to sin, both the nation and its king would be destroyed.

■ *The elderly prophet/judge Samuel addressed*
■ *the nation of Israel publicly for the last time in*
■ *his career. The focus of his final speech was a*
■ *condemnation of the people for their desire to*
■ *trust in an earthly king more than in a heav-*
■ *enly King. He encouraged them to return to a*
■ *sincere trust in God and warned them that if*
■ *they failed to do so, God would destroy both*
■ *their nation and their king.*

SAUL DISOBEYS GOD AND FORFEITS
HIS PROMISE OF A DYNASTY (13:1–15)

Saul's Army (vv. 1–4)

When Saul was a young man (The NIV's "thirty
years old" is only a guess. The Hebrew actually
says he was "one year old."), he became king
and ruled "forty" (Acts 13:21, NIV, says
"forty-two"; Hebrew says "two years") years.

Israel's most persistent and threatening enemy
during Saul's day were the Philistines. In an
effort to drive them out of the territory of Benjamin, Saul assembled a force of three thousand
soldiers to attack the Philistines. Two thousand
were under the king's command, and another
thousand were placed under his son Jonathan's
control.

Philistine Response (vv. 5–7)

Learning of Saul's activities, the Philistines sent
a huge force of three thousand chariots, six
thousand horsemen, and multitudes of ground
troops to Micmash in the Benjamite area to challenge him. When Saul's soldiers observed the
size of the Philistine force, many of them panicked and abandoned the army: some hid in
caves and tombs in the area, while others went
east of the Jordan to get away.

Saul's Disobedience (vv. 8–14)

Obeying Samuel's previously given directions,
Saul and the remaining troops camped at Gilgal
for seven days, awaiting the prophet's arrival
before going into battle. When on the seventh
day it seemed that Samuel was not coming, Saul
began performing prebattle sacrificial rites that
should have been carried out by Samuel. Just as

the king was finishing the task, Samuel arrived. Seeing that Saul had disobeyed the divinely inspired orders to wait, Samuel proclaimed an oracle to the king. In it he indicated that Saul's dynasty, one which could have lasted throughout all of Israel's history, had now come to an end. The Lord had selected a nonfamily member to reign after Saul.

Saul's Change of Plans (v. 15)

Following this tense confrontation between prophet and king, Saul abandoned his plans to attack the Philistines that day and returned instead to his hometown of Gibeah. Only six hundred troops were still with him at this time.

■ *Saul fielded an anti-Philistine attack force of*
■ *three thousand men, which he deployed in*
■ *the territory of the tribe of Benjamin. The*
■ *Philistines responded with a counterforce so*
■ *large that many of Saul's soldiers abandoned*
■ *him.*
■   *Though Saul had been prophetically*
■ *warned not to go into battle for a*
■ *week—until the prophet Samuel could offer*
■ *up sacrifices—Saul became impatient and*
■ *afraid and offered up the sacrifices himself.*
■ *As a penalty for his disobedience, God took*
■ *away the king's opportunity to have his heirs*
■ *sit on Israel's throne.*

JONATHAN LEADS ISRAEL TO VICTORY OVER THE PHILISTINES (13:16–14:23)

Israel's Advantage (13:16–23)

Saul, Jonathan, and Israel's troops redeployed to Geba, near Saul's capital city of Gibeah, while the Philistine force set up their camp at nearby

One of the most sinister aspects of sin is that it never affects only one person. Saul sinned by performing a ritual sacrifice that only Samuel was qualified to offer. This act of disobedience hurt Saul's kingship, but it also took something precious away from his children. They lost the right to rule Israel after their father.

The choices we make in life really do matter. Not only do they enrich or threaten our own lives, but they also affect the lives of those around us. Our obedience to God brings blessings to our families. By the same token, our disobedience pulls others around us down, keeping them from inheriting all the blessings that otherwise could have been theirs. What blessings are lost to your family members because of your sins? How can you live to bring more blessings to others around you?

Micmash. The Philistines then split up their troops into three divisions, apparently to prevent the Israelite army from using key roads around Gibeah. Israel's enemy possessed a crucial advantage at this time, for only they had blacksmiths and, therefore, the ability to make iron weapons.

Jonathan's Victory (14:1–15)

Without his father's knowledge, Jonathan and a slave left the Israelite camp to scout out one of the Philistine camps. When he arrived at the Philistine outpost, God gave him a sign indicating that he could attack the Philistines. Climbing up a steep cliff to get to the Philistines, Jonathan and his slave arrived at the top, skirmished with the Philistines, and killed about twenty men.

Jonathan's victory stunned the Philistines, who took this as a sign of divine displeasure. That impression was strengthened by an earthquake that also struck central Israel on that day.

Philistines Routed (14:16–23)

When Saul's scouts reported unusual activity in the Philistine camp, the king mustered his troops and discovered Jonathan's absence. Without waiting to obtain divine guidance, Saul sent the Israelite army into battle. The Israelites routed the Philistines that day.

Jonathan's tactics in this fight with the Philistines defied military logic. He found an established enemy outpost that had a superior strategic position—a camp on top of a steep hill, approached it, and then revealed his position to the enemy. When the enemy invited him to fight, he climbed the steep hill— thereby exposing himself to attack and exhausting himself. Amazingly, God not only protected Jonathan in this encounter but gave him a great victory as well. Truly, faith won the victory on that day!

■ *The Israelite army camped just outside of*
■ *Gibeah, and the Philistines camped nearby.*
■ *When the Philistines broke up their main*
■ *camp in order to trap the Israelites, Jonathan*
■ *and a slave secretly scouted out and then*
■ *attacked one of the minor Philistine outposts.*
■ *When Jonathan killed twenty men at about*
■ *the same time an earthquake took place—a*
■ *sign of divine displeasure, all the Philistine*
■ *encampments became panicky. Panic turned*
■ *into a massive defeat, as Saul led Israel's*
■ *forces against them.*

1 SAMUEL 15

SAUL IS REJECTED AS ISRAEL'S KING (15:1–35)

Holy War (vv. 1–9)

The prophet Samuel came to Saul and revealed that the Lord was ordering the king to initiate a holy war (see *Holman Bible Dictionary* article: "War") against the Amalekites because of wrongs they had done to Israel during the days of Moses. God ordered the Israelites to kill all the Amalekites and their livestock in this holy war. Saul called up an army of 210,000 men, led them just beyond Israel's southern border, and attacked the Amalekites there. Israel handed the Amalekites a crushing defeat. However, the Israelites under Saul's command failed to fulfill the Lord's command. They kept alive Amalek's king Agag, as well as the best livestock they captured.

Saul's Fear and Disobedience (vv. 10–25)

The Lord informed Samuel of Saul's disobedience and expressed regret that Saul had ever been made king. The elderly prophet was deeply disturbed by this and set out to confront the king about his sin. He caught up with Saul at Gilgal and asked why he had disobeyed God's commands. Saul initially denied any disobedience but later admitted his failure to carry out the divinely ordained mission. Saul's fear of his troops, a fear which exceeded his fear of God, led him to commit this sin.

"Behold, to obey is better than sacrifice and to heed than the fat of rams" (1 Sam. 15:22b, NASB).

God's Rejection of Saul as King (vv. 26–29)

As punishment for this sin, God announced that He was rejecting Saul as king over Israel. Saul begged the prophet for forgiveness and asked the prophet to accompany him as he returned to his troops for a victory sacrifice. However, Samuel refused and turned to leave. Saul, who needed Samuel's support to keep a firm grip on Israel's kingship, threw himself down before the prophet and desperately grabbed the old man's robe in an effort to make him stay; in the process he tore the prophet's robe. In response Samuel proclaimed that God had torn kingship from Saul and given it to one more worthy than Saul.

Samuel's Last Visit with Saul (vv. 30–35)

When Saul again asked the prophet for forgiveness and help, Samuel agreed to return to the military camp with the king for one final appearance with him. There Samuel executed the Ammonite king, finishing the business Saul had left undone. Never again would Samuel visit Israel's king, though he grieved deeply for Saul.

- As a culmination of his ongoing pattern of
- sin, Saul disobeyed the Lord's guidelines for
- fighting a holy war against the Amalekites.
- As a result, the Lord permanently rejected
- Saul as king.

QUESTIONS TO GUIDE YOUR STUDY

1. What were two ways in which Saul disobeyed God?
2. What were the consequences for both Saul and his family?

1 SAMUEL 16

THE LORD SELECTS DAVID TO SUCCEED SAUL (16:1–13)

Samuel's Search for a New King (vv. 1–10)
Sometime after this event God sent Samuel on the risky mission of anointing a successor to a sitting king. The prophet was sent to the Judahite family of Jesse to designate one of his sons as God's choice as Israel's next king. Journeying southward, Samuel arrived in the unwalled rural village of Bethlehem. There he held a sacrifice attended by Jesse's family. Though the prophet initially tried to anoint Jesse's oldest son Eliab, God prevented him from doing so.

David's Anointing (vv. 11–13)
When God also rejected every other son of Jesse at the event, the puzzled prophet asked if Jesse had any other sons. Jesse told him about David, his youngest son who was tending the family flock. David had apparently been excluded from the event because he was too young for

Throughout the Old Testament narratives, God showed His tendency to "color outside the lines" of human expectations. Ancient near eastern societies always gave special privileges—especially leadership roles—to firstborn sons. However, in the biblical stories, God regularly chose people who were overlooked and ignored by others to do His most special work. In the events of 1 Samuel 16, David joins a long line of other individuals who were honored by God, even though they had been disqualified by people because of their birth order. Abraham, Isaac, Jacob, Joseph, Ephraim, and Moses were also younger brothers whom God exalted over their peers.

military service—a key part of an Israelite king's responsibility (see 1 Sam. 8:20). In response to the prophet's request, David was summoned. God made known that David was His choice to be Israel's next king. When the young man was anointed, God's Spirit came upon him mightily.

■ *In obedience to God's command, Samuel*
■ *anointed Jesse's youngest son David to serve*
■ *as Israel's second king.*

DAVID SERVES KING SAUL (16:14–23)

Saul's Evil Sprit (vv. 14–17)

At the time David received God's Spirit, Saul lost it. Replacing the divine Spirit in Saul's life was an evil spirit that tormented him. Saul's servants recognized the change in the king's life and recommended that he seek relief from someone who could drive the evil spirit away.

David as Armor Bearer (vv. 18–23)

Ironically, the person chosen to drive away Saul's evil spirit was David, who used his musical skills as a harpist to provide temporary relief to the troubled king. David was so effective at helping Saul that the king made him a regular member of the royal court, bestowing on him the title of armor bearer, a position that may have been customarily filled by capable young men not yet old enough for military service.

The Old Testament links Israel's great musical heritage with the life of David. Seventy-three of the psalms are credited to David—more than six times the number attributed to any other person or group. David was both a performer and a writer of music. He was also responsible for making music a central part of Israelite temple worship; he made the Levitical clans of Asaph, Heman, and Jeduthun the permanent musicians charged with the responsibility of making music a major part of the worship of God at Jerusalem (see 1 Chron. 25).

■ *David, newly empowered with God's Spirit,*
■ *used his abilities as a harpist to deliver king*
■ *Saul from the power of an evil spirit.*

29

DAVID DELIVERS ISRAEL FROM A PHILISTINE GIANT (17:1–58)

Goliath, the Giant (vv. 1–16)

Fifteen miles west of David's hometown of Bethlehem in the Valley of Elah the Philistines set up a military camp. Saul led a force of Israelites into that region to hold them in check, setting up a camp within eyeshot of them. At first, neither side attacked the other. Instead, the Philistines challenged the Israelites to have one soldier fight a giant named Goliath to the death. The nation whose contestant died would serve—that is, pay taxes to, the winner's nation. Goliath, who was over nine feet tall, well armed, and protected by heavy armor, taunted the Israelites for forty days; but none of Saul's soldiers dared to fight him.

David's Willingness to Face Goliath (vv. 17–40)

One day David was sent by his father to bring provisions to three of his older brothers serving with Saul. David heard Goliath's taunts and, though heckled by his brothers, volunteered to meet the giant in a battle to the death. At first King Saul rejected David's offer; but after hearing of David's earlier acts of bravery and his great faith in God, he gave the young man permission to face Goliath. For protection, Saul offered to let David wear the royal armor and use the king's weapons, but David refused. Instead, he went into battle wearing no armor, carrying only a sling for a weapon, but trusting fully in God for victory.

The Bible does not state how large the rock was that David used against Goliath. Typical sling stones in the ancient Near East were about the size of tennis balls and weighed about a pound apiece.

Goliath's Death (vv. 41–51a)

After exchanging words with Goliath, David ran toward him and slung a single stone. The stone caught the Philistine in the forehead and immediately felled him. David then grabbed Goliath's sword and cut off the fallen giant's head.

Philistine Retreat (vv. 51b–58)

Realizing that their hero was dead, the Philistine forces immediately retreated, followed in close pursuit by the Israelites. Many Philistines were killed during the headlong race back to their cities. After the battle, David's family was rewarded with a tax-exempt status, and David was given the right to marry a royal princess.

- *The Philistine army encamped in Israelite*
- *territory, and Saul led the Israelites to con-*
- *front them. A forty-day standoff occurred*
- *when no Israelite soldier dared to take up the*
- *Philistine giant Goliath's challenge to settle*
- *the dispute by fighting him to the death. The*
- *stalemate was broken when David, the newly*
- *anointed youngest son of Jesse, bravely*
- *fought and killed Goliath, thus inspiring*
- *Israel to a great victory over the Philistines.*

QUESTIONS TO GUIDE YOUR STUDY

1. Whom did God choose to be the second king of Israel, and how?
2. What roles did David play in Saul's administration?

SAUL BECOMES JEALOUS OF DAVID AND TRIES TO KILL HIM (18:1–30)

David's Success in Battle (vv. 1–5)

On the day that David killed Goliath, Saul made David a permanent part of his royal household. Saul's oldest son Jonathan became best friends with David and confirmed this special friendship by giving the young hero royal clothing and weapons. Saul regularly sent David to do battle against the Philistines; and David enjoyed great success, a fact that led Saul to give the underage soldier a high rank in the Israelite army.

Saul's Jealousy (vv. 6–16)

Saul changed his attitude toward David. However, when he noticed that the people celebrated David's feats more than the kings' in their songs, he feared David would usurp the throne. When an evil spirit attacked Saul not long after that, David was sent in to play music to soothe the king. But Saul used the occasion to try twice to kill David with a spear. With the Lord's help, David escaped both times. In spite of Saul's attacks, David continued to serve as a victorious military commander in Saul's army.

Saul's Efforts to Kill David (vv. 17–30)

In an effort to bring about David's death on the battlefield, Saul offered David a chance to marry the king's first daughter Merab. To claim the prize, however, David would have to bring proof that he had killed one hundred Philistine soldiers (literally, present the king with one hundred foreskins). David did not fear the challenge, but he felt unworthy to marry Israel's

David's willingness to remain in the room long enough for Saul to throw a spear at him twice (18:11) portrayed the incredible depth of David's loyalty to the king and his commitment to helping Saul overcome his torments. What kinds of risks are you willing to take to help others?

most prestigious royal princess and so turned down the offer. However, when the king offered him the opportunity to marry the younger princess Michal, David accepted the terms. Soon he presented the king with two hundred Philistine foreskins and thus became Saul's son-in-law. As a result, Saul's fear of David grew, and David became the king's lifelong enemy.

- *As a commander in Israel's army, David*
- *enjoyed great success in battle against the*
- *Philistines. While this initially pleased Saul,*
- *the king came to fear David. He tried to kill*
- *David, but his efforts backfired. David ended*
- *up marrying the king's daughter Michal and*
- *becoming best friends with the king's oldest*
- *son Jonathan.*

1 SAMUEL 19

SAUL TRIES OTHER WAYS TO KILL DAVID (19:1–24)

Orders to Kill David (vv. 1–6)
His previous efforts having failed, Saul ordered all his slaves, as well as his son Jonathan, to kill David. However, since David was Jonathan's best friend, instead of obeying his father, he told David about his father's intentions and tried to talk his father out of an attack on David.

Plots to Kill David (vv. 7–17)
For awhile Jonathan's efforts worked. However, one day Saul became tormented by an evil spirit, and David was called in to play his harp and help the king. Saul used the occasion to try

Michal helped David escape by putting a *teraphim*, an idol, in David's place in bed. Teraphim were abominable to the Lord (see 1 Sam. 15:23), and Michal's use of one here, even for a noble purpose, suggests that she was a spiritual rebel.

to kill David with a spear. When that failed, he sent men to capture and kill David at his house the next morning. Michal learned of her father's plan and used a deceptive tactic to help David escape during the night.

Protection for David (vv. 18–24)

David's flight from the royal palace brought him to Samuel's residence at Ramah. When Saul learned of David's whereabouts, he sent three separate squads of soldiers to Naioth at Ramah to arrest David. However, each time the Spirit of God protected David by forcing all the soldiers to do nothing but prophesy. Frustrated by all of this, Saul finally went to capture David himself. Yet the king, too, was overpowered by God's Spirit. Not only did Saul prophesy, but he also removed his royal clothing and lay down in Samuel's presence for an entire day and night.

■ *Saul intensified his efforts to kill David. The*
■ *king attempted to use his slaves, his oldest*
■ *son, his soldiers, and his own efforts to kill*
■ *David. All these attempts failed, however, in*
■ *part because God's Spirit miraculously inter-*
■ *vened to protect David.*

"Is Saul also among the prophets?" was a popular proverb in the early days of Israel's monarchy related to a dimension of King Saul's life that had caught many by surprise. Earlier in his life, Israel's first king was so spiritually dark that his slave had to tell Saul that God could help him with his problems (see 1 Sam. 9:6). Then Saul thought that prophets needed to be paid before they would provide help from God (see 1 Sam. 9:7). Saul also did not recognize the most famous spiritual leader of his day (see 1 Sam. 9:18). Yet when God got control of Saul's heart, a new dimension was added to his life. To everyone's surprise, Saul began to prophesy (10:11). This phenomenon reached a peak during the events of this chapter.

DAVID AND JONATHAN MAKE A LOYALTY COVENANT (20:1–42)

David's Visit with Jonathan (vv. 1–23)

Following Saul's journey to Naioth, David left Samuel and went to visit Saul's son Jonathan to try to understand the king's murderous motivations. At first Jonathan was stunned to hear about his father's plot to kill David and refused to believe it. But David devised a plan to show Jonathan the king's true intentions, and together they worked out a way to help David escape permanently from the royal household—if escape was necessary. The two young men also made a binding promise to be eternally loyal to each other and to each other's family members.

The Plot to Uncover Saul's Anger (vv. 24–34)

In the scheme involving Saul, David would be absent from meals at the royal table that he was supposed to attend. Jonathan's role in the matter was to mislead his father regarding the real reason David was not present. David missed meals with Saul two days in a row, and Saul asked Jonathan why this was so. Jonathan provided an excuse for David, and Saul became angry, accusing Jonathan of siding with David against the king. In his rage Saul threw his spear at Jonathan, hoping to kill him.

Parting of Friends (vv. 35–42)

Jonathan, now convinced that Saul wanted to murder David, left the palace and went to an agreed-upon rural location to pass the word along to David. Using the flight of an arrow to symbolize David's need to flee from Saul, Jonathan informed David of his danger. A tearful

According to the Torah, Israelites were to offer up a sacrifice on the first day of a lunar cycle (see Num. 29:6). A ritual meal would normally be associated with this event (v. 5), but only ritually clean persons could eat such a meal (Lev. 7:20–21). Because normal daily activities such as marital relations or even touching certain insects could cause ritual uncleanness, Saul's suspicions were aroused only when David was absent from a meal that did not require ritual cleanness.

private meeting between the two friends marked the last time they would ever meet before David became a permanent fugitive from Saul.

- Saul's son Jonathan learned that his father
- intended to murder David. Instead of sup-
- porting his father in the matter, however, he
- made a lasting pledge of loyalty to David and
- helped him escape.

1 SAMUEL 21–22

DAVID BEGINS HIS LIFE AS A FUGITIVE (21:1–22:5)

Priestly Assistance (21:1–9)

David left Samuel to seek help from another member of the tribe of Levi, Ahimelech the priest at Nob. Ahimelech had not expected a visit from David and trembled when he came. He thought this soldier's solitary visit to the holy site must mean there was trouble in the kingdom. David tried to put the priest at ease by telling him the king had ordered David to lead a hastily arranged secret mission. Then he asked Ahimelech for food and a weapon. Ahimelech gave him some holy bread of the Presence, food normally reserved for priests. But in keeping with the Law of Moses' principle of acting to sustain life, David was given what he wanted. David also received Goliath's sword, a weapon which David had apparently dedicated previously to God at Nob. Doeg, an Edomite servant of Saul, observed David's actions at Nob.

Jesus referred to this incident in David's life (see Matt. 12:3–4 and parallels), using it as an illustration of compassionate flexibility in the application of the Torah's rules and to assert His own claims to being Lord of the Sabbath.

David's Flight to Gath (21:10–15)

In his search for personal safety, David sought refuge from Saul by fleeing to Gath, a walled Philistine city beyond Saul's grasp. However, the Philistines knew nothing of Saul's fear of David. They also feared David greatly and believed he had come to Gath only to destroy them. When David observed their reaction to his coming, he acted shrewdly to avoid capture and death at the hands of the Philistines. He pretended to be insane, leading his would-be killers to shun him and let him live.

Continued Flight (22:1–5)

Leaving Philistine territory, David returned to the tribal territory of Judah, hiding out in the cave of Adullam. David's family, as well as about four hundred Israelite men, joined him there. Then David left Judah, leading the group to Mizpah in Moab. There he asked the Moabite king to grant asylum to his parents, but David and his group did not stay in Moab. When the prophet Gad warned David to leave this enemy nation's territory, they did so.

The Torah severely restricted Israelite contacts with Moab (see Deut. 23:3–6). It was probably Gad's concern to help David avoid violating these restrictions that motivated him to leave Moab and return to Israel.

■ *To help David in his escape from Saul, David*
■ *asked for and received food and Goliath's*
■ *weapon from Ahimelech the priest at Nob.*
■ *David then spent short periods of time in Phi-*
■ *listia and Moab before returning to Israelite*
■ *territory in Judah. In the process, some four*
■ *hundred Israelite men joined forces with*
■ *David.*

SAUL SLAUGHTERS THE PRIESTLY CITY OF NOB (22:6–23)

Saul in Gibeah (vv. 6–10)

Saul was holding court under a tamarisk tree in the royal city of Gibeah. When he was informed that David and his men had been discovered, he became angry that his own family and servants were not providing him with the help needed to kill David. After the king's tirade, Doeg the Edomite, a foreigner serving at court, informed Saul that David had recently received guidance, food, and a weapon from Ahimelech the priest at Nob.

David's Loyalty (vv. 11–15)

When Saul heard this, he immediately ordered all the priests at Nob to appear before him at court. Once there, Saul accused them of helping David lead a revolt against the king. Ahimelech admitted he had helped David but denied that David was involved in any sort of rebellion against the throne. To the contrary, David was Saul's most loyal subject.

Saul's Revenge (vv. 16–23)

Saul refused to believe Ahimelech's defense of David and pronounced the entire city of Nob guilty of treason. He then ordered the immediate execution of every priest of the Lord at Nob. Saul's Israelite servants refused to kill God's priests, but the foreigner Doeg the Edomite obeyed the command fully. Eighty-five priests, along with their families and animals, died that day. All of the slain citizens had been relatives of Eli the priest, who had had a curse placed on his family line because of sinful behavior in a previous generation (see 1 Sam. 2:32–33). Only one priest—Abiathar—escaped with his life. He fled to David and found refuge with him in the desert.

- ■ *Saul falsely accused his family and servants*
- ■ *of disloyalty to him. Then in a moment of*
- ■ *insane rage, he ordered the execution of*
- ■ *eighty-five priests of the Lord along with*
- ■ *their families and animals for their role in an*
- ■ *imagined revolt against the king. Of the*
- ■ *priests who were targeted for death, only*
- ■ *Abiathar escaped. He joined David's group.*

Doeg's complete destruction of all living beings in Nob was carried out according to a severe form of war guidelines known as *herem*, or "ban" warfare. The Israelites were authorized to use this form of war only against the worst offenders of the Lord's holy laws (see Exod. 22:20; Num. 21:2–3; Deut. 7:1–2). Doeg's use of the ban against Israelite priests was particularly offensive.

1 SAMUEL 23

DAVID ESCAPES FROM SAUL NEAR ZIPH (23:1–29)

Victory over Philistines (vv. 1–6)

While in the desert regions of Judah, David learned that the Philistines were looting the threshing floors of the nearby Judahite city of Keilah. David desired to help his fellow Israelites, so he sought the Lord's will about it, apparently with the aid of the Urim and Thummin that were part of Abiathar's priestly ephod (see *Holman Bible Dictionary*, s.v. "ephod"). Through Abiathar, God told David to lead his forces to victory against the Philistines. David attacked the foreign invaders, defeated them soundly, and saved the people of Keilah.

Last Visit with Jonathan (vv. 7–18)

King Saul learned of David's exploits at Keilah and called up all his forces to capture David there. Before Saul got to Keilah, however, David learned of the king's plans and with Abiathar's help asked God for guidance in responding to the threat. God warned David that he must leave Keilah or face certain capture. David obeyed God and led his troops—now numbering about six hundred men—away from Keilah to the desert strongholds near the Judahite city of Ziph. At the desert stronghold of Horesh, David's best friend Jonathan—Saul's oldest son—secretly visited him, bringing encouragement and a renewed pledge of loyalty. This meeting marked the last time David ever saw his friend alive.

Rock of Parting (vv. 19–29)

The Ziphites informed Saul that David and his men were staying near their city. The king then led his troops to the region in pursuit of David. When David moved his men farther south into the Judahite desert, Saul's troops followed. The king finally caught up with David in the desert of Maon and sent his troops around the hill occupied by David and his men. Before he could engage David in battle, however, a messenger reached the king, informing him of an outbreak of Philistine attacks on Israelite settlements. Saul was forced to withdraw from David in order to confront the Philistine threat. David and his men named the location of their close encounter with Saul "Sela Hammahlekoth" ("Rock of Parting") and left for En Gedi, site of an oasis in the rugged hills west of the Dead Sea.

En Gedi (lit., "Spring of the Young Goat") is a major oasis on the western side of the Dead Sea, about thirty-five miles southeast of Jerusalem. It is the best source of fresh water in the wilderness area immediately west of the Dead Sea.

■ *Though a fugitive, David loyally defended*
■ *the Israelites from the Philistines. When Saul*
■ *came to fight David in the desert regions of*
■ *Judah, God repeatedly helped David avoid*
■ *confrontations with the Israelite army.*

DAVID SPARES SAUL'S LIFE AT EN GEDI (24:1–22)

An Opportunity to Kill Saul (vv. 1–7a)

After finishing the skirmish with the Philistines, Saul was informed that David and his men were encamped at En Gedi, a spring in the rugged hills west of the Dead Sea. In response, Saul led a group of three thousand soldiers to that region to capture his son-in-law. Once there, Saul went into a cave alone some distance away from his troops to relieve himself (see Deut. 23:12). Ironically, David and a group of his soldiers were hiding in the very location chosen by Saul. Saul's awkward private moment provided David a golden opportunity to kill Saul, and his men urged him to do so. David refused, however, because Saul was God's chosen ("anointed") leader over Israel and to kill him would be tantamount to defying God. But David did secretly cut off the corner of Saul's robe as a means of proving to the king that he could have been killed.

Momentary Truce (vv. 7b–22)

Saul, who was unaware of any of this, left the cave. David then called out to the king from the entrance to the cave and bowed down and confirmed his loyalty to him. Saul was humbled and deeply moved by David's actions and words. Weeping, Saul admitted that David was more righteous than he and that David would one day become king of Israel. In exchange for a solemn promise from David that he would never wipe out Saul's family line, Saul withdrew his troops and returned to Gibeah. Not believing that Saul had really ended his quest to kill David,

According to Numbers 15:38–39, Israelites were required to have tassels on the corners of their robes that served as reminders of the Law and their obligation to obey it. By cutting the tassel from Saul's garment, David removed Saul's reminder to follow God's Law and made the garment technically in violation of the Torah. Apparently, it was David's realization that he had interfered with an anointed king's ability to fulfill the Law of God that caused him grief in this matter.

David, however, and his men remained in the desert regions of Judah.

■ *When Saul pursued David at En Gedi, he*
■ *almost lost his life. However, though David*
■ *could have killed Saul when the king was*
■ *alone in a cave, David showed his respect for*
■ *God and the king by sparing the king's life.*
■ *When Saul learned of David's mercy, he*
■ *praised David, secured a promise of protec-*
■ *tion for his family line, and withdrew his*
■ *troops.*

QUESTIONS TO GUIDE YOUR STUDY

1. Why did Saul turn against David?
2. How did David respond to Saul's threats on his life?

1 SAMUEL 25

DAVID DEALS WITH WICKED NABAL AND MARRIES ABIGAIL (25:1–44)

David's Anger (vv. 1–13)

The name *Nabal* literally means "intellectual/moral fool." In light of Nabal's behavior, the name is certainly appropriate (see v. 25).

At this time, Samuel died and was buried with honor at his hometown of Ramah. Following the funeral, David and his troops moved into the central Judahite wilderness near Maon. There they protected the vast herds of Nabal, a wealthy Judahite, from Philistine raids and predatory animals. At sheep-shearing time—perhaps in the spring or fall, David sent messengers to Nabal to request some compensation. However, Nabal refused and insulted David and his men in the process. David responded with impulsive anger, summoning his troops to kill all the males of Nabal's clan.

Abigail's Pleas (vv. 14–35)
Nabal's beautiful wife Abigail learned of David's troop movements and, in violation of normal rules of conduct for a woman in the ancient Near East, hastily went out to confront David and plead for her husband's life. Abigail warned David to leave revenge to God, suggesting that David's headstrong actions in the present matter could damage his career. David was so impressed by Abigail's actions, words, and accompanying gift of food that he returned to his camp without taking revenge on Nabal.

Nabal's Death (vv. 36–38)
Meanwhile, Nabal was getting drunk at a great feast. Abigail returned home to tell her husband about the recent events but could not since he was drunk. When she spoke to him the next day, Nabal suffered an apparent stroke and slipped into a coma. He died ten days later.

David's Marriage to Abigail (vv. 39–44)
David learned about Nabal's death and came to understand the value of leaving vengeance to God. He then sent messengers to Nabal's widow Abigail, offering to marry her and thus provide her with lifelong care. She accepted David's proposal. David had previously married Ahinoam of Jezreel. Before that he had lost custody of his wife Michal. Saul had forced her to marry Paltiel, an otherwise unknown Israelite.

Wealthy Nabal cheated David and his troops by not paying them for the protection provided to him, his shepherds, and his flocks. David's first reaction to Nabal's sin was to "get even." He would kill Nabal and every other man associated with him. This impulsive, hotheaded response is easy to understand. Nabal's refusal to compensate David and his men for their work meant that David's army might suffer or even die of hunger in the desert. However, David's initial decision to get personal revenge against Nabal was wrong.

Long before David's time God had said, "It is mine to avenge; I will repay" (Deut. 32:35, NIV). As Nabal's brave and wise wife Abigail indicated, if David carried out his foolish plan to kill Nabal, he would have to live with a guilty conscience for the rest of his life. Instead of inheriting blessings from God, David would become the focus of God's judgment. David soon learned that God can be trusted in the matter of righting wrongs through vengeance.

■ *Though a fugitive from Saul, David used his*
■ *troops to protect Israelite interests, in this*
■ *case the wealth of Nabal, well-to-do Juda-*
■ *hite. When Nabal tried to cheat David,*
■ *Nabal's wife Abigail persuaded David not to*
■ *retaliate but to leave vengeance to God. Ten*
■ *days later Nabal died of natural causes.*
■ *David married Nabal's widow.*

1 SAMUEL 26

DAVID SPARES SAUL'S LIFE A SECOND TIME (26:1–25)

Saul's Pursuit of David (vv. 1–4)

The Ziphites, people from David's own tribe of Judah, went to King Saul, informing him that David's troops were hiding out in their area. Accordingly, Saul led his expeditionary force of three thousand men to the Desert of Ziph. David and his men were safely hidden from the king, however.

David in Saul's Camp (vv. 5–11)

One night, after Saul and his troops had bedded down for the night, David and his cousin Abishai secretly entered Saul's camp. David proceeded to the spot where Saul, surrounded by his soldiers and his commander Abner, was sleeping. Abishai asked David for permission to kill Israel's king immediately, but David did not permit Saul to be harmed because God had chosen Saul to be Israel's king (see 1 Sam. 24). God might choose to kill Saul as punishment for his sins against David, but David would not be the one to take the king's life.

Saul's Affirmation of David (vv. 12–25)

To help teach Saul a lesson, however, David took Saul's spear and water jug, located near the king's head. Then without awakening anyone David and Abishai left the camp and crossed over to a nearby hill. In the darkness David started shouting loudly, taunting Saul's commander Abner. Saul was awakened by the commotion and recognized David's voice. In a short conversation between David and his father-in-law the king, Saul admitted he had sinned and acted foolishly by trying to kill David. He also blessed his son-in-law and prophesied that he would one day triumph.

The next day Saul withdrew his troops from the area. Never again does the Bible indicate that Saul attacked David.

■ *King Saul once again went out in the Juda-*
■ *hite desert to hunt down David. However,*
■ *David not only avoided capture but actually*
■ *sneaked into Saul's military camp one night*
■ *and stole the king's spear and water jug.*
■ *Convinced that David had no intentions of*
■ *ever killing him, the king admitted his own*
■ *wrongdoing and no longer attempted to kill*
■ *David.*

DAVID FINDS REFUGE AMONG THE PHILISTINES (27:1–12)

The End of Saul's Pursuit (vv. 1–4)

David realized that in spite of Saul's sincere words the only way to prevent the king from pursuing him was for David and his troops to leave Israelite territory. Accordingly, David, his six hundred men, and their families moved to the Philistine city of Gath under the protection of King Achish, who now recognized David as an enemy of Saul and therefore a potentially valuable ally for the Philistines. David's actions proved effective, for Saul permanently suspended his search for David.

David in Ziklag (vv. 5–9)

At the same time David realized that living in Goliath's hometown also posed a serious threat to his safety. Wisely therefore, David requested and received permission to settle his group in Ziklag, an unimportant rural village in the general vicinity. In return for Achish's protection, David's group was expected to make some sort of contribution to the Philistines' welfare. This was done by David leading his troops in deadly raids to gain loot for the Philistine government.

David's Conquests (vv. 10–12)

In periodic reports to King Achish, David claimed he was attacking Israelite settlements. However, in truth David was attacking traditional enemies of Israel living in semidesert regions not far from Philistine territory, killing all the inhabitants of Geshurite, Girzite, and Amalekite towns, and then seizing their flocks and goods. Achish, who was no doubt

Israel had failed to eliminate all the original inhabitants from Canaan during the days of Joshua and the Judges (see Judg. 2:20–23). While at Ziklag, David and his men spent their days secretly destroying enemies of Israel that had never been driven out of Judahite territory. Even in exile, David remained focused on doing the Lord's work.

impressed with the gifts David brought him, believed David's lies. He concluded that because of these raids David had become deeply hated by the Israelites and would, therefore, become a gift-bearing servant of the Philistines forever. What David was actually doing, however, was continuing the God-given task of conquering the Promised Land for Israel.

■ *To protect his group against the lingering*
■ *threat of King Saul, David moved his family,*
■ *all his troops, and their families to Philistine*
■ *territory. Achish, king of Gath, gave David*
■ *and his men the rural village of Ziklag to live*
■ *in, in exchange for goods plundered from*
■ *nearby non-Philistine settlements. David*
■ *deceived Achish, making him think he had*
■ *stolen the goods from Israelites. In actuality,*
■ *he had taken them from Israel's enemies.*

1 SAMUEL 28

SAUL SEEKS MILITARY GUIDANCE WITH A MEDIUM'S HELP (28:1–25)

New Conflict Between Israel and the Philistines (vv. 1–4)

The Philistines, Israel's most threatening enemy at this time, once again gathered their forces to fight Israel. This time they set up camp at Shunem, preparing to do battle with Israel in the territory of Manasseh. Since David was under the protection of the Philistines, King Achish of Gath informed David that he and his troops would have to participate in the battle against Israel.

Saul's Search for God's Guidance (vv. 5–6)

When King Saul became aware of the Philistines' troop movements, he led Israel's troops to Gilboa, not far from the Philistine camp. Before going forth into battle, however, Saul sought divine guidance. Getting a word from God was not easy, since Samuel was now dead and Saul had alienated himself from the Lord's priests (see 22:6–19). Furthermore, God did not give the king any meaning-laden dream, nor was a prophet found who could reveal God's will to the king.

The Medium of Endor (vv. 7–19)

Scholars are divided on the question of whether Samuel actually spoke to Saul during the seance. Some suggested alternatives include the following: (1) The medium actually roused Samuel. (2) God, not the medium, sent Samuel to Saul. (3) A demonic/satanic deception occurred. (4) The medium faked the apparition. (5) The experience was actually a hallucination. A surface reading of the text suggests Samuel actually spoke to Saul.

Saul's desperation to get authoritative advice led him to seek the help of a woman living in nearby Endor who was a medium, a person who held seances to speak with the spirits of dead people. When Saul did this, he violated God's Law revealed to Israel at Mount Sinai, which imposed the death penalty on everyone who consulted mediums (see Lev. 20:6). Ignoring this threat, however, in the middle of the night, Saul ordered the medium to summon the spirit of the prophet Samuel. A spirit claiming to be Samuel arose from the ground and spoke with the king. However, instead of providing Saul with guidance in fighting the Philistines, it reminded Saul of his disobedient past and announced that the king, his sons, and many Israelite soldiers would die in battle the next day.

Preparation for Battle (vv. 20–25)

Saul fell to the ground in terror when he heard these words. However, the medium and his soldiers helped him regain his composure. After eating a sumptuous meal prepared for the king by the medium, Saul and his men returned to the Israelite military camp to await the events of the following day.

■ *The Philistines amassed troops at Shunem*
■ *to fight Israel in the tribal territory of*
■ *Manasseh. Saul responded by leading the*
■ *Israelite army to that region. Before fighting,*
■ *however, Saul sought divine insight for battle*
■ *from the dead prophet Samuel with the aid of*
■ *a medium, a practice strictly forbidden in the*
■ *Law of Moses. For this sinful act the spirit of*
■ *Samuel told Saul that he, his sons, and troops*
■ *would die in battle the next day.*

1 SAMUEL 29

DAVID IS PROHIBITED FROM FIGHTING WITH THE PHILISTINES (29:1–11)

Assembly at Aphek (vv. 1–5)

In preparation for the expected battle with Israel, the Philistine commanders assembled a large force at Aphek, a military staging site near Philistine territory that had plenty of water, grain fields, and places to camp. In accordance with Achish's request, David and his men joined the Philistines there. When the other Philistine commanders learned that Israelites, especially an infamous Philistine killer, were among their group, they became angry with Achish. As a result, Achish was forced to dismiss David and his men from the Philistine army.

March to Battle (vv. 6–11)

David must have secretly breathed a sigh of relief at this turn of events, yet he publicly expressed indignation that he would not be permitted to "fight against the enemies of my lord the king" (v. 8, NIV). David's words were delightfully ambiguous. Was David's "lord the king" Achish, Saul, or God? The reader, who already knows David's heart, suspects that David would have turned his forces against the Philistines on the battlefield. Nevertheless, David's group would have no opportunity to do that. Instead they got up early the next morning and began the southerly three-day trek back to Ziklag, just as the Philistine army moved north on a three-day march to Jezreel to meet Saul.

■ *When the other Philistine commanders*
■ *learned that Achish had enlisted David*
■ *and his forces in their army, they angrily*
■ *demanded that David and his men be*
■ *removed from their ranks. David was thus*
■ *spared from having to fight against Saul and*
■ *the Israelites. His group left for Ziklag just as*
■ *the Philistines moved forward to do battle*
■ *against Saul.*

1 SAMUEL 30

DAVID BATTLES AMALEKITE MARAUDERS (30:1–30)

Destruction of Ziklag (vv. 1–6)

At the end of three days David and his troops arrived back at Ziklag. When they arrived, however, they were horrified to discover the city abandoned and destroyed. Amalekite soldiers had plundered the village, kidnapping everyone in it and then burning it to the ground. The families of David and all his men were missing, and the grief of David's men soon turned to rage against David. They spoke of rising up in mutiny against their leader and killing him.

Pursuit of the Amalekites (vv. 7–10)

Before the men could act, however, David consulted God to determine what should be done to get the missing people back. God promised David and his men success if they would pursue the Amalekites. Accordingly, David and his six hundred men set out after them. However, one third of the troops—two hundred men—were too exhausted to keep up the pace and were allowed to drop out of the pursuit.

Victory over the Amalekites (vv. 11–20)

While tracking the enemy, David's remaining men found a slave abandoned by the Amalekites. The man, an Egyptian, was treated kindly by David and, in exchange for safety, led David's forces to the Amalekite camp. The men attacked and furiously fought the Amalekites for two days, destroying all but four hundred of them. Afterward they recovered all missing Israelite women and children, in addition to seizing the Amalekites' flocks and herds.

David's rule regarding the equal distribution of booty finds its parallel in Paul's teaching about Christian service: one plants, another waters, but all are equal, and all are rewarded (1 Cor. 3:6–9).

Rules for the Army (vv. 21–25)

A dispute arose among David's men when the booty was being divided up after the conflict. At first the men who actually did battle with the Amalekites refused to give any booty to the two hundred soldiers who remained behind. However, David used the occasion to establish a permanent rule followed by Israelite armies ever since that time: All soldiers, regardless of their position in the army, would share equally in the rewards.

Booty for Israel (vv. 26–30)

David also sent generous portions of the booty to Israelite leaders in the region of Judah. These gifts were designed to make it easier for David and his men to return to Israel following their now imminent departure from Philistine territory.

■ *Returning to Ziklag after being excluded from*
■ *the Philistine army, David and his men discov-*
■ *ered their village had been burned and their*
■ *families kidnaped by the Amalekites. With*
■ *God's help, David's forces attack and defeat the*
■ *Amalekites, thus saving their families and*
■ *gaining much booty in the process.*

1 SAMUEL 31

THE PHILISTINES DEFEAT ISRAEL; SAUL AND HIS SONS DIE (31:1–13)

Death of Saul (vv. 1–6)

At the time David's troops were fighting the Amalekites, the Philistines attacked Saul and the Israelites southwest of the Sea of Galilee on Mount Gilboa. The battle turned into a tragic massacre as the Philistines killed many Israelite soldiers, including three of King Saul's sons—Jonathan, Abinadab, and Malki-Shua. Saul, likewise, was seriously injured by a Philistine archer. As the enemy approached to capture, humiliate, and then kill him, Saul ordered his armor bearer to kill him first. However, the

During their Exodus from Egypt under Moses' leadership (ca. 1446 B.C.), the Israelites were viciously attacked in the desert by the Amalekites. With Joshua leading the Israelite forces, however, the Israelites successfully defended themselves against their foes. After the battle, Moses prophesied that the Lord would one day wipe out the Amalekites (see Exod. 17:8–16).

In this section of 1 Samuel we see David being used by God to act on that ancient prophecy. So complete was David's destruction of the Amalekites that they are never again mentioned in either the books of Samuel or Kings.

The Philistines Defeat Israel; Saul and His Sons Die (31:1–13)

young man refused, since doing so would mean killing God's chosen leader. In desperation Saul then fell on his own sword, whereupon the armor bearer did the same.

Saul's Burial (vv. 7–13)

The next day the Philistines returned to the battlefield to remove all objects of value from the Israelites' dead. At that time they discovered the corpses of Saul and his three sons. Cutting off their heads and stripping them, the Philistines took the bodies and hung them on the walls of the recently captured town of Beth Shan. Israelites from Jabesh Gilead learned of the Philistines' shameful treatment of Saul and his sons and decided to risk their lives to do something about it. One night some soldiers from Jabesh Gilead secretly removed the remains of the royal family and gave them a dignified burial.

- *The Philistines massacred Israel at Jabesh*
- *Gilead, bringing about the death of King*
- *Saul and three of his sons. The noble citizens*
- *of Jabesh Gilead provided a dignified burial*
- *for the slain royal family members.*

QUESTIONS TO GUIDE YOUR STUDY

1. How did Saul learn that he would die?
2. When was the destruction of the Amalekites first prophesied?

Soon after Saul became king, he had mobilized an Israelite army to help the Jabesh Gileadites fight against the Ammonites (see 1 Sam. 11:1–11). Saul's valiant efforts saved the city, and its citizens never forgot what he had done for them. The tragic circumstances of 1 Samuel 31 provided a fitting opportunity for the Jabesh Gileadites to pay a final tribute to the one who had rescued them.

53

DAVID LAMENTS THE DEATHS OF SAUL AND JONATHAN (2 SAM. 1:1–27)

The News of Saul's Death (vv. 1–16)

Scholars are divided in their opinions as to whether the Amalekite was lying when he claimed to have killed Saul. Some believe the Amalekite's words in 2 Samuel 1 supply additional details to the account of Saul's death in 1 Samuel 31. Others believe he lied in order to try to claim a reward from David.

After returning triumphantly with their families to what was left of Ziklag, David and his troops spent two days recovering from their battle with the Amalekites. Their tranquillity was shattered the third day by a visit from an Amalekite who had just come down from Mount Gilboa, the site of Saul's death. Appearing before David, the young foreigner provided him with a dramatic account of Saul's death. In his description, the Amalekite claimed personal responsibility for ending Saul's life. To lend credibility to his story, he presented Saul's personal jewelry to David. The young man had expected David to reward him for killing the man who had been pursuing David. Instead, David ordered the Amalekite's death because he had dared to kill the Lord's chosen leader over Israel.

Tribute to Saul (vv. 17–27)

Then David the warrior-musician composed a song that paid tribute to the life and careers of Saul and his son Jonathan. The emotionally charged lyrics commanded the Philistines not to rejoice in their destruction of Israel's king and ordered the mountain on which Saul died to become a dry, barren wilderness. At the same time the song praised Saul and Jonathan and ordered the Israelite women to grieve over their untimely deaths. The poem concludes with an intensely personal section in which David expressed a personal sense of loss created by the death of his best friend Jonathan.

- David learned of the deaths of Saul and
- Jonathan. The Amalekite who claimed per-
- sonal responsibility for putting an end to the
- king's life was killed by David, who then
- composed a mournful song to commemorate
- Saul's and Jonathan's deaths.

2 SAMUEL 2–3

DAVID BECOMES KING OF JUDAH (2:1–3:1)

Hebron, the New Capital (2:1–4a)

After Saul's death, David saw an opportunity to return safely to Israel. By consulting the Lord, David and his troops learned they were to relocate to the Levitical city of Hebron, in the southern regions of the territory of Judah. The leaders of David's ancestral tribe came to that city to anoint him king over that tribe, and Hebron was established as David's capital city.

Opposition to David (2:4b–11)

After becoming king over one tribe, David began the difficult task of winning the support of the rest of Israel, an undertaking that would take seven years and six months. He began by making a gesture of peace to the Jabesh Gileadites. Leading the opposition to David was Abner, the commander of Saul's troops, who anointed Saul's forty-year-old surviving son Ish-Bosheth king over the rest of Israel. With Abner's help, Ish-Bosheth then set up Mahanaim, a city east of the Jordan, as his capital city.

Battle of Rival Kings (2:12–16)

Tensions were high in Israel because of the presence of two rival kings in the land. The tensions soon sparked a civil war. The actual killing began when the rival kings' troops encountered each other near Saul's old capital city of Gibeon. Twenty-four men—twelve from each force—battled to the death there.

Increased Conflict (2:17–3:1)

A broader conflict broke out immediately after that initial encounter. David's forces prevailed that day (19 deaths versus 360 for Ish-Bosheth's troops), but not before Abner had killed Asahel, the brother of David's commander Joab. Enraged by his brother's death, Joab led his troops to pursue Abner's forces, with the intention of killing them all. Some calming words by Abner to Joab prevented further bloodshed, however.

Abner first warned Asahel not to fight with him, then urged him to arm himself before fighting. When Asahel persisted, Abner killed Asahel with the butt-end of a spear (v. 22), a circumstance that suggests he was defending himself—not attacking—when the death occurred. Later, Asahel's brother Joab would be killed for murdering Abner in revenge (see 1 Kings 2:5, 31–34).

■ *Following Saul's death, David was anointed*
■ *king over Judah, one of the twelve tribes of*
■ *Israel, while Ish-Bosheth, Saul's remaining*
■ *son, became king over the rest of the land.*
■ *From his capital city of Hebron, David began*
■ *a bloody seven-year campaign that would*
■ *ultimately result in his becoming king over*
■ *all Israel.*

QUESTIONS TO GUIDE YOUR STUDY

1. Following Saul's death, how long was it before David became undisputed king over all Israel?

2. Who was a rival king to David for some of this time?

ABNER TRIES TO HELP DAVID BECOME KING OF ALL ISRAEL (3:2–39)

David's Sons (vv. 2–5)

While David was king of Judah at Hebron, he fathered six sons by six different wives. The increasing number of wives reflects David's growing influence and prestige. Amnon was David's oldest son and heir apparent, while Absalom was his third born.

Scriptures indicate that David had at least eight wives and ten concubines and fathered at least twenty sons and one daughter (see 2 Sam. 3:2–5; 5:14–16; 12:15; 13:2; 15:16; 1 Chron. 3:5–8).

Peace Between Rivals (vv. 6–16)

Toward the end of the struggle between rival kings, Ish-Bosheth's commander Abner came to play a leading role in the Saulide forces. Ish-Bosheth, who probably felt threatened by his commander's power, accused him of sleeping with Rizpah, one of Saul's concubines. Abner became so enraged he vowed to help make David king of the land. Making good on his word, Abner informed David of his intentions. David was wary of his former opponent and demanded some proof of his sincerity. Abner would have to return David's first wife Michal, who had previously been taken from David by Saul (see 1 Sam 25:44). Accordingly, Abner forced Michal to leave Paltiel and go to David.

Plans for David's Anointing (vv. 17–21)

To help assure David's acceptance by the people of Israel and especially the tribe of Benjamin, Abner met with leaders from these groups. Having successfully lobbied in David's behalf, Abner went to Hebron to share the good news, then left to make arrangements for David to be anointed by these tribes.

Abner's Death (vv. 22–27)

Before he could return to Israel, however, Abner was intercepted by Joab's men, who tricked him into a deadly encounter with David's military

Hebron was a city of refuge (see Josh. 20:7; 21:3), a location where it was illegal to avenge the death of anyone without a trial first. Joab's murder of Abner in Hebron was thus a double crime.

commander. To avenge the death of his brother Asahel, Joab murdered Abner in Hebron.

Mourning for Abner (vv. 28–39)

David's chances of becoming king over all Israel were severely threatened by Abner's murder. Attempting to control the damage, David arranged for a large state funeral to honor Abner and ordered his soldiers, beginning with Joab, to mourn for their dead opponent. David's efforts succeeded, and the rest of Israel did not blame Abner's death on David.

■ *As David continued to grow in prestige and*
■ *power in Judah, Ish-Bosheth's regime fell*
■ *apart when Abner defected to David. How-*
■ *ever, Abner was murdered by Joab before he*
■ *could finish the task of making David king of*
■ *all Israel.*

2 SAMUEL 4

ISH-BOSHETH IS MURDERED (4:1–12)

Support for David (vv. 1–6)

When Ish-Bosheth learned that Abner had switched his support to David, he and all his supporters panicked, realizing that his days as king over Israel were almost over. Sensing the turning tide, Recab and Baanah, two of Ish-Bosheth's military captains, followed Abner's lead and turned against Ish-Bosheth as well. However, unlike Abner, they kept their decision secret until they had acted treacherously.

Death of Recab and Baanah (vv. 7–12)

While Ish-Bosheth was sleeping one afternoon, the two men crept into the king's residence at Mahanaim, entered his bedroom, and decapitated him. Taking his head with them, Recab and Baanah then fled west across the Jordan, hastening to David at Hebron. They hoped that the Judahite king would reward them for killing Ish-Bosheth. However, David condemned their act and pronounced them guilty of murder. The king then ordered his soldiers to seize and kill Recab and Baanah. This done, their bodies were then mutilated and desecrated. Ish-Bosheth's head was respectfully placed in the tomb of his great-uncle Abner.

Ish-Bosheth is known elsewhere as Eshbaal ("the fire of Baal"); Mephibosheth is known elsewhere as Merib-Baal ("Baal is contending"). The names were apparently changed by the biblical writer in order to eliminate the name of a pagan god in the Holy Scriptures. In its place, he substituted the term meaning "shame." This scribal habit is found only in 1, 2 Samuel and may have been done in order to fulfill God's command not to place the name of a pagan on their lips (see Exod. 23:13).

■ *Following Abner's decision to support King*
■ *David, Ish-Bosheth was murdered by two of*
■ *his own soldiers. The men went to David to*
■ *attempt to collect a reward for killing the*
■ *rival king, but David tried them for murder*
■ *and had them executed.*

2 SAMUEL 5

DAVID BECOMES KING OF ALL ISRAEL AND ESTABLISHES A NEW CAPITAL (5:1–25)

The Beginning of David's Rule of All of Israel (vv. 1–5)

With both Abner and Ish-Bosheth dead, leaders of all the tribes previously unwilling to support David came to him at Hebron and agreed to make him their king. Thus, at age thirty David was anointed king of all Israel. In all, David would rule over Israel a total of forty years—seven and one-half years while at Hebron and thirty-three years while at Jerusalem.

Jerusalem Conquered (vv. 6–8)

David's first reported act as king was to conquer Jerusalem. The Jebusites, who inhabited the city, taunted David by claiming that even the blind and lame could successfully defend the city from David's attack. However, the resourceful Israelite king had his troops sneak through an underground passageway leading from a water source outside Jerusalem to the interior of the city. He conquered the city and made it his capital.

Growth in Jerusalem (vv. 9–16)

David did much to build up Israel's new capital city. He added fortifications, increased the hilltop city's usable building area by constructing sturdy terraces around the edge of the settlement, and built a palace with assistance from Hiram, king of Tyre. David's successes in Jerusalem were paralleled by a growing family. Eleven named sons, including Solomon, were born to David during his years at Jerusalem.

Battle at Baal-Perazim (vv. 17–25)

As the newly anointed king of all Israel, David represented a major threat to the Philistines. They mobilized all their forces to capture him, but he escaped to a stronghold. Following God's guidance, David then attacked and defeated the Philistines at Baal-Perazim and the Valley of Rephaim.

- *Following Ish-Bosheth's death, all Israel*
- *anointed David king at Hebron. David then*
- *successfully led Israel's forces to victory*
- *against the Jebusites and the Philistines. In*
- *the process, David conquered the city of*
- *Jerusalem and made it Israel's capital.*

David's success in capturing the Jebusite city of Jerusalem met two important objectives: First, it helped Israel fulfill God's command to conquer the Promised Land; and second, it provided David with a neutral site for a new capital city. Jerusalem's location made it the ideal administrative center for the newly united nation since it was situated on the border between Judah and the northern tribes. When Jerusalem became home to the ark of the covenant, the city became the place where God caused His name to rest (see Deut. 12:5, 11, 21).

2 SAMUEL 6 · · · · · · · · · · · · · · ·

DAVID BRINGS THE ARK OF THE COVENANT TO JERUSALEM (6:1–23)

Jerusalem—Home of the Ark (vv. 1–5)

David desired to make Israel's new capital city the nation's religious center as well. Accordingly he mobilized a force of thirty thousand special troops for the purpose of bringing the ark of the covenant safely from Baalah of Judah (otherwise known as Kiriath Jearim) to Jerusalem, to reside in a special tent David had prepared for it. In David's special group were members of the priestly tribe of Levi, who were responsible for actually transporting the ark.

Guidelines for Moving the Ark (vv. 6–7)

Unfortunately, the Levites Uzzah and Ahio disobeyed God's guidelines for moving the ark, the throne of God. They carried it on an oxcart instead of their shoulders. Near Jerusalem the oxen pulling the cart stumbled, causing the ark to jostle. Uzzah feared the ark would fall, and so he grabbed it. For this, God instantly killed him because only Aaronic priests were allowed to touch it (see Num. 4:20).

61

The ark of the covenant was constructed approximately four hundred years prior to David's time and was Israel's holiest object. It was a gold-covered wooden box about four feet long, two-and-a-half feet wide, and two-and-a-half feet deep. It had a golden lid, the mercy seat, with two cherubim on top, and was provided with two carrying poles. Only an Aaronic priest was permitted to view it. When being transported publicly, it had to be covered with cloth and leather (see Exod. 25:9–22; Num. 4:19–20).

The Ark in Jerusalem (vv. 8–15)

This tragedy both angered David and made him afraid. The king immediately halted the procession and ordered that the ark be placed in the nearby home of Obed-Edom. To mark the event, he named the site Perez-Uzzah ("outbreak against Uzzah"). Three months later, David renewed his attempt to bring the ark to Jerusalem, and this time succeeded because the Levites followed the divinely prescribed procedures.

Celebration for the Ark (vv. 16–19)

As the ark was entering Jerusalem, there was boisterous music and celebration. David danced before the Lord at the head of the procession, and a great crowd of men and women accompanied the ark. The ark was placed in a special tent; special animal sacrifices were made; and everyone attending the event was given a generous food gift.

Michal's Criticism (vv. 20–23)

Noticeably absent from the celebration was David's wife Michal, who severely criticized David for his lively participation in the event. David defended his actions. Apparently as a result of her rejection of God and David, Michal remained childless throughout her lifetime.

■ *After a failed first attempt, David succeeded*
■ *in bringing the ark of the covenant, God's*
■ *earthly throne, to Jerusalem. David rejoiced*
■ *in the ark's arrival. His wife Michal criti-*
■ *cized David's actions, and as a result, expe-*
■ *rienced the curse of childlessness throughout*
■ *her lifetime.*

THE LORD MAKES A PROMISE TO DAVID (7:1–29)

A Temple for Jerusalem (vv. 1–5)

After David was well established as king over all Israel—a time perhaps several years after the events of chapter 6, David told the prophet Nathan he wanted to build a Temple for the Lord in Jerusalem. At first Nathan encouraged David to undertake the project. However, when Nathan was alone the Lord told him otherwise.

A Kingdom for David (vv. 6–16)

Through the prophet Nathan, the Lord told David that he had never asked for a building in which to reside and did not want David to construct one now. Turning the tables, God promised to "build a house" for David—that is, to make David the founder of a dynasty that would continue forever. David's descendants would always sit on Israel's throne, and God's unfailing love would never be taken away from them. One of David's son would be given the privilege of building a Temple in Jerusalem.

The Greatness of God (vv. 17–29)

Nathan conveyed the divine promises to David, and David accepted them gratefully. He marveled that God had taken him from an unpromising background to give him this incredible promise. David then expressed profound wonder at God's greatness: The Lord was a miracle-working God who had helped Israel in the past and had made Israel His forever. David confessed that all God's words are true; thus, these divine promises could be trusted.

The New Testament writers and Jesus Himself understood the promises God made to David in 2 Samuel 7 to be fulfilled in the person and work of Jesus Christ. Jesus was the ultimate Son of David and eternal King (see Matt. 1:1; 2:2; 21:5; 27:11, 37).

■ *God prohibited David from building a house*
■ *for the Lord in Jerusalem but promised to*
■ *make David the founder of an unending*
■ *dynasty. David rejoiced in these promises*
■ *and gave thanks to God for them.*

QUESTIONS TO GUIDE YOUR STUDY

1. Where did David live following Saul's death?
2. What city did David eventually establish as the capital city?
3. What promise did God make to David when He didn't allow him to build the Temple?

2 SAMUEL 8

DAVID CONQUERS ISRAEL'S ENEMIES (8:1–18)

Conquest over Gath (vv. 1–2)

King David continued his assault on the Philistine nation in an impressive manner when he led Israel in the conquest of the Philistines' largest city, Gath. David also led Israel's forces to conquer Moab, one of the countries just east of Israel. In an effort to limit the Moabites' ability to war against Israel in the future, David killed two thirds of the Moabite prisoners of war.

David's Victories (vv. 3–11)

Turning Israel's armies to the north, David won victories against the armies of the city-states of Zobah and Damascus. Following these conquests, David decimated their armies and military equipment and took much valuable booty—especially quantities of gold and bronze. An additional benefit of David's victories was the establishment of relations with the northern city-state Hamath. In appreciation of David's defeat of Hamath's enemies, their king sent David gifts of gold, silver, and bronze. David in turn gave the gifts and booty to God, apparently to be used for the construction of the new Temple.

In 1 Chronicles 2:14, David stated that he had acquired about four thousand tons of gold, nearly forty thousand tons of silver, and even greater amounts of iron and bronze to be used in constructing the Temple. Most of this vast amount would have come from his conquests.

Conquered Foes (vv. 12–14)

Additionally, David won victories over the Arameans (or Edomites?), Ammonites, and Amalekites. Indeed, God gave David victories against every foe he fought.

David's Leadership (vv. 15–18)

David's governmental and military administration was headed up by a small group of men who had proven themselves capable in their service to the king. Included among his highest ranking leaders were his own sons, whom he sanctioned as priests (NIV, "royal advisors").

■ *As king over all Israel, David led the nation*
■ *to victory against the Philistines and*
■ *Moabites, as well as Aramean city-states, the*
■ *Ammonites, and Amalekites. David gave the*
■ *material benefits gained from these wars as*
■ *gifts to God. David also established a stable*
■ *governmental administration which*
■ *included his own sons.*

2 SAMUEL 9

DAVID FULFILLS HIS PROMISE TO JONATHAN AND SAUL (9:1–13)

Care for Saul's Family (vv. 1–4a)

One of David's concerns as king over Israel was to fulfill a promise he had made to members of the house of Saul. David had vowed to care for the children of Jonathan, should anything happen to Jonathan. Now that Jonathan was dead and David's own situation had stabilized, it was time to act. Accordingly, David summoned Ziba, one of Saul's former slaves—perhaps his chief slave—to the royal palace and quizzed him concerning the whereabouts of any survivors of Saul's family.

Saul's Grandson (vv. 4b–13)

David learned that Mephibosheth, Jonathan's crippled son and Saul's grandson, was living in exile east of the Jordan River. Immediately he sent servants to bring Mephibosheth to Jerusalem. Mephibosheth was afraid when he was called before David because he was uncertain of the treatment he might receive. However, David spoke kindly to him and restored to his family all of his grandfather Saul's possessions. The king also had Mephibosheth and his son Mica move to Jerusalem as permanent, personal guests at the royal court. Ziba and his clan were then ordered to serve as Mephibosheth's slaves and, care for the property Mephibosheth had inherited from his grandfather Saul.

A gruesome tradition in ancient western Asia was for founders of new royal dynasties to murder every member of the previous ruling family (see 2 Kings 10:1–11; 11:1). David chose not to do this, however. Keeping a promise he had made to two dead friends, David defied typical logic and gave Mephibosheth, a direct descendant of King Saul, a position of privilege at the royal palace in Jerusalem. Questions would arise later about Mephibosheth's loyalty to David, but no one would doubt David's loyalty to Jonathan and Saul.

■ *David fulfilled a commitment made to Saul*
■ *and Jonathan years earlier by bringing*
■ *Jonathan's surviving son and grandson,*
■ *Mephibosheth and Mica, to Jerusalem to be*
■ *treated as permanent guests in the royal*
■ *household.*

2 SAMUEL 10

DAVID DEFEATS THE AMMONITES (10:1–19)

Strife with the Ammonites (vv. 1–3)

Some time later Nahash king of the Ammonites, an ally of David, died. To express sympathy and to affirm the covenant between Israel and Ammon, David sent a delegation to Nahash's son Hanun. Perhaps trying to use this occasion to break the nation's ties with Israel, Hanun's advisors convinced him that David's ambassadors were actually military spies.

Declaration of War (vv. 4–7)

Accordingly, Hanun decided to insult the visitors and the nation they represented by shaving off half their beards and cutting off their robes at the buttocks. When David learned of this humiliating act against Israel, which amounted to a declaration of war, he was not slack in taking up the challenge.

In anticipation of an attack by Israel, the Ammonites hired thirty-three thousand mercenaries and positioned them to defend their nation. For his part David sent Joab with the entire Israelite army against Ammon.

The Ammonites Routed (vv. 8–14)

On the battlefield Joab split his troops into two groups—one under his leadership and one under his brother Abishai's—to handle simultaneous attacks from the Ammonites and their allies. The strategy proved successful, and Israel routed the Ammonite coalition.

Ammonites Defeated (vv. 15–19)

In response, the Ammonites increased the number of mercenaries fighting for them and prepared for another fight. For this second battle David personally led Israel's troops and won a decisive victory, killing more than forty thousand of the enemy. As a result, the Ammonites became subject to Israel.

- *Following the death of King Nahash, the new*
- *Ammonite king insulted an Israelite ambas-*
- *sage. As a result two military encounters*
- *between Israel and Ammon ensued, with*
- *Israel winning both of them. Ammon thus*
- *became subject to Israelite control.*

QUESTIONS TO GUIDE YOUR STUDY

1. What did David do with the booty from his military conquests?
2. How did David demonstrate his faithfulness to the family of Saul and Jonathan?

DAVID SINS AGAINST BATHSHEBA AND URIAH (11:1–27)

David and Bathsheba (vv. 1–5)

The following spring, David sent Israel's army out to attack the Ammonites' capital city of Rabbah. Joab led the army while David tended to business in Jerusalem. One evening David spent some time on the flat porchlike roof of his palace in Jerusalem. From that vantage point he watched Bathsheba, the beautiful wife of his valued soldier Uriah, as she took a ritual bath in a public bathing area in the city. Then in a shocking disregard for the Lord's Commandments, David ordered Bathsheba brought to his palace, where he committed the capital crime of adultery. Afterward the woman was sent home. Not many days later, Bathsheba sent word to David that she was pregnant.

Plot of Uriah's Death (vv. 6–17)

Panicked by this news, David hatched a plot to disguise his sin. Bathsheba's husband Uriah was urgently summoned back to Jerusalem from Rabbah. David made it appear that Uriah had returned in order to give the king information regarding the Ammonite war. In truth, however, David did this so that Uriah could have a time of intimacy with his wife and thus become the apparent father of the child. But Uriah refused to disobey standard Israelite military rules, which prohibited soldiers from becoming ritually unclean through sexual contact during military operations. Because Uriah would have no marital intimacy with his wife at this time, David took the desperate measure of sending him back to Ammon, carrying a secret order for

Why was David in Jerusalem when his soldiers were fighting the Ammonites? It was probably to protect him, Israel's most valuable citizen, from the dangers of the battlefield (see 2 Sam. 21:17). Furthermore, at this time his armies were besieging Rabbah, a process that could take months or years. He would only be needed on the battlefield when the siege was ending.

Joab to arrange for Uriah to die on the battlefield. Joab followed the king's orders, and Uriah died fighting the Ammonites.

Care for a Military Widow (vv. 18–27)

After learning of Uriah's death, David brought Bathsheba into his harem. In the course of time, she gave birth to a son. Israelites who were ignorant of David's sin would have viewed these events with satisfaction since it seemed as if the king was merely caring for a valiant soldier's widow and then raising up an offspring in behalf of the dead man (see Ruth 4). Though many Israelites were probably fooled by David, God was not. The Lord was displeased with David's actions.

■ *While his army was busy fighting the Ammo-*
■ *nites one spring, David stayed in Jerusalem*
■ *where he committed adultery with Bath-*
■ *sheba, wife of one of his soldier's, thereby*
■ *causing her to become pregnant. To cover his*
■ *sin, David had the soldier killed; then he*
■ *married the widow.*

2 SAMUEL 12

DAVID IS CONFRONTED WITH, AND CONFESSES, HIS SIN (12:1–31)

Nathan's Rebuke (vv. 1–12)

The Lord directed the prophet Nathan to go to David and rebuke him for his sin. Nathan confronted David skillfully, using a story about a rich man who stole a poor man's sheep to guide the king into condemning his own sinful

In the ancient Near East, kings would not fight wars during every season of the year. Large armies, such as those described in the Bible—ones with soldiers often numbering in the hundreds of thousands, required huge amounts of food and water. It was impractical or impossible for the armies to bring all their food supplies along with them from their homeland, so they would wait until the grain fields in the area of conflict were ripe. The army would then feed its troops with grain stolen from the enemy's fields.

Barley, the grain crop that would ripen first, was ready to harvest in the spring in the Middle East. In addition, the rainy season was over at this time and would not start again until the fall. Thus, with its better weather and abundant food supply, spring was the time when kings would go to war.

actions. When David pronounced judgment against the rich man in the story, Nathan indicated that David himself was actually that man. He then proclaimed that God would bring death and rebellion to David's household because of the king's sin.

David's Sorrow (vv. 13–14)

Jolted by the prophet's rebuke, David immediately confessed his sin. God accepted David's sorrowful words and indicated that because of David's repentant act he would not have to die for the sin. However, the baby born as a result of David's sinful union would perish.

David's Son's Death (vv. 15–23)

David was deeply disturbed by this ominous prophecy and began fasting in an effort to save the infant's life. However, in spite of David's sincere efforts, the boy died seven days after being born. When David learned of his son's death, he solemnly accepted it, ceased his fasting, changed his clothes, and went to the tabernacle to worship God.

Solomon's Birth (vv. 24–25)

Not long afterward David went to Bathsheba to comfort her. She soon became pregnant and in due time became the mother of a second son. The child's parents named him Solomon, while the prophet Nathan proclaimed his name to be Jedidiah, "beloved of the Lord."

Victory over Rabbah (vv. 26–31)

While all of this was going on, Joab continued to lead Israel's troops in a siege of Rabbah, the Ammonite capital city. Just before the city fell, Joab told the king to hasten to the battlefield if he wanted to be able to take credit for the victory. David did so, taking in the process many slaves and much booty, including a seventy-five

According to the Torah, the penalty for adultery is death (see Lev. 20:10). The fact that the repentant David did not have to die for his sin with Bathsheba is a testimony to God's merciful grace. Have you experienced God's forgiving grace in your life?

Psalm 51 records David's passionate prayer for forgiveness for the sins he had committed against Bathsheba and Uriah. He pleaded for God to "wash away" all his iniquity and "cleanse" him from his sin. He confessed that God is able to forgive him and make him "whiter than snow."

pound (one talent) crown. The Ammonite slaves were later used as a labor pool to support Israel's public building projects.

■ *Through the prophet Nathan, God rebuked*
■ *David for his sin and pronounced severe*
■ *judgments on David's household. Though*
■ *David confessed his sin, Bathsheba's new-*
■ *born son died. Later Bathsheba and David*
■ *had a second child named Solomon. David*
■ *also completed the conquest of Ammon at*
■ *this time.*

QUESTIONS TO GUIDE YOUR STUDY

1. What were David's strategies in covering his sin with Bathsheba?
2. What was David's reaction to Nathan's confrontation with him?

2 SAMUEL 13 · · · · · · · · · · · ·

DISASTER STRIKES DAVID'S HOUSEHOLD: RAPE AND MURDER (13:1–39)

Amnon and Tamar (vv. 1–5)

David's oldest son Amnon became infatuated with his virgin half sister Tamar, the sister of Absalom. Amnon was so strongly attracted to her that he became sick when she refused his advances. With the help of his cousin Jonadab, Amnon devised a scheme that would permit him to steal Tamar's virginity.

The Rape of Tamar (vv. 6–14)

Amnon pretended to be sick. When his father King David came to visit him, Amnon asked his father to order Tamar to prepare him a special meal to help him get better. David complied with his son's request, and Tamar entered Amnon's residence to prepare the meal. Once there, Amnon arranged for her to enter his bedroom alone and then raped her.

Absalom named his daughter Tamar, apparently after his sister (see 2 Sam. 14:27). Perhaps he did this as a gesture of consolation since his sister would never be able to marry and have children herself.

Amnon's Hatred (vv. 15–19)

Immediately after Amnon committed the crime, he felt intense hatred toward Tamar and ordered his slaves to throw her out of the apartment. Tamar was devastated by the event and with good cause. Her loss of virginity meant that she was essentially disqualified from ever being given in marriage to another man; and Amnon, the one man who could have married her, would have nothing to do with her. Thus she would probably never be able to bear children and would have to live for the rest of her days in shame.

Absalom's Revenge (vv. 20–22)

Tamar's protective brother Absalom helped to comfort her and made arrangements for her to live in his household under his protection. Absalom also hatched a plot to avenge his half brother Amnon's crime.

Amnon's Death (vv. 23–31)

To carry out his plan, Absalom manipulated his father, King David, into forcing Amnon to attend a celebration associated with the shearing of Absalom's sheep. At the festive meal associated with the event, Absalom got his half brother drunk and then ordered his slaves to murder him. When Amnon died, the rest of the guests at the party fled in panic, and in the confusion

David received a report that Absalom had murdered all the king's sons.

David's Grief (vv. 32–39)

Though the more drastic account proved false, David was deeply grieved because of the untimely death of Amnon, who was his first-born son and heir apparent.

Meanwhile, Absalom fled from the royal household in Jerusalem, seeking refuge with his grandfather Talmai, king of Geshur. He stayed there three years, during which time David's desire to be reconciled with Absalom intensified.

■ *God's promise of terrible judgment against*
■ *David's household began to be fulfilled by a*
■ *series of three events: David's oldest son,*
■ *Amnon, raped his half sister Tamar. Amnon*
■ *was murdered by Tamar's brother Absalom.*
■ *Absalom went into a self-imposed exile away*
■ *from Jerusalem.*

2 SAMUEL 14

ABSALOM RETURNS FROM EXILE (14:1–33)

Forgiveness for Absalom (vv. 1–22)

Though Absalom had murdered his half brother, David still loved his son and wished to see him again. Nevertheless, because of the crime Absalom had committed, the king refused to permit him to return to Jerusalem. Joab knew David's heart and thought it in David's best interest to let Absalom return. Accordingly, Joab hired a wise woman from Tekoa who came before the king, pretending to be the mother of a son who had murdered his brother. The woman pretended that her relatives were threatening to kill her only living son because of his crime. To prevent this, the woman begged David to issue a royal edict sparing the murderer's life. When David agreed to do this, the woman immediately asked him why he refused to act so forgivingly toward his own son Absalom. Confronted by the woman in this way, David decided to permit Absalom to return to Jerusalem. The king then sent Joab to Geshur to end Absalom's exile.

When David issued an edict in the incident for the wise woman of Tekoa, he was fulfilling his royal responsibilities to act as a judge over Israel (see Ps. 72:1–2). He was also taking up the cause of widows (see Deut. 27:19; Isa. 1:17).

Return to Jerusalem (vv. 23–33)

Absalom was permitted to return to Jerusalem but only on the condition that he never be allowed to see his father. For two years Absalom lived in Jerusalem under these terms, but it frustrated him greatly to do so. When he could take it no longer, he requested a visit from Joab to discuss the matter. When Joab repeatedly refused to come to Absalom, the king's son ordered his slaves to burn Joab's barley field. The strategy worked, for Joab immediately went to Absalom. After discussing the field, Absalom asked Joab to get David to change his policy—either let the king kill Absalom or exonerate him.

Joab brought Absalom's request to David; and after five years of external and internal exile, Absalom was at last permitted to see his father. When he entered the king's presence, David symbolically expressed his acceptance of his son by kissing him.

Absalom was at that time a handsome man and the father of four——three sons and one daughter. He was also hairy. During his annual haircut, he would lose five pounds of hair.

■ *With Joab's help, David changed his attitude*
■ *toward Absalom, at first permitting his son*
■ *to return to Jerusalem, then granting him full*
■ *acceptance and forgiveness.*

2 SAMUEL 15

ABSALOM PROCLAIMS HIMSELF KING; DAVID FLEES JERUSALEM (15:1–37)

The Bible does not state why David's counselor Ahithophel joined the effort to overthrow the king. Perhaps it was because David had committed adultery with Ahithophel's granddaughter Bathsheba and ordered the death of her husband Uriah (see 2 Sam. 11:3; 23:34).

Absalom's Effort to Be King (vv. 1–6)
Once Absalom regained his previous status in David's family, he began taking steps to replace David as king of Israel. Acquiring horses, a chariot, and a private militia, Absalom also began positioning himself to become David's replacement as the highest legal authority in Israel. His efforts paid off. He became more popular than his father throughout Israel.

Absalom as King (vv. 7–12)
After four years Absalom decided it was time to fulfill his ambitions by proclaiming himself king over Israel. At a ceremony in Hebron, the city of his birth and David's first capital city, Absalom was anointed king; and people throughout Israel supported him. Among his followers was David's most prized counselor, Ahithophel, the grandfather of Bathsheba. Absalom then took steps to occupy Jerusalem.

Flight from Jerusalem (vv. 13–31)

When David learned of his son's treasonous actions, he feared for his life. Hastily he ordered all the members of his royal court—except for ten concubines, who were to keep the palace in order—to abandon Jerusalem and go into exile east of the Jordan River. Among the loyalists who accompanied David were his royal bodyguard (the Kerethites and Pelethites) and six hundred soldiers from Gath. Zadok and Abiathar, Israel's leading priests, offered to go with David and bring the ark of the covenant with them; but David refused to let them come along. Instead he asked them to return to Jerusalem and act as spies.

Hushai, the Spy (vv. 32–37)

David also ordered his valued adviser Hushai to go back, with the hope that Hushai could provide Absalom with bad advice, as well as spy on him. Hushai obeyed David and pretended to join Absalom's rebellion. Meanwhile, Absalom and his forces occupied Jerusalem.

■ *Four years after being reconciled with his*
■ *father, Absalom declared himself king at*
■ *Hebron and took steps to topple David from*
■ *power in Jerusalem. David and a group of*
■ *loyal followers escaped the royal city just*
■ *before Absalom could catch him.*

DAVID FLEES AS ABSALOM RAPES DAVID'S CONCUBINES (16:1–23)

Mephibosheth's Hope to Be King (vv. 1–4)

While fleeing eastward, David and his group were met by Mephibosheth's head slave Ziba just outside of Jerusalem on the Mount of Olives. There Ziba provided the group with two donkeys and a generous food gift. When quizzed by David about his master, Ziba stated that Mephibosheth hoped to use the present crisis to make himself king. David immediately disinherited Mephibosheth, giving his estate to Ziba instead.

Insults for David (vv. 5–14)

As David's group continued their eastward trek toward the Jordan River, they passed the Benjamite village of Bahurim. There Shimei, a relative of King Saul, loudly insulted David and threw stones and dirt at the group. Abishai, one of David's generals, offered to kill Shimei, but David prevented it, suggesting that God may have told Shimei to say what he did.

It was customary for kings to assume rights over the harem of their predecessors (see 2 Sam. 12:8). Absalom's outrageous act against David's concubines was designed to reinforce his claim to David's throne.

Concubines Raped (vv. 15–23)

As David was fleeing, Absalom and his followers were entering Jerusalem. Greeting him there was Hushai, who offered his services as a royal counselor. Absalom's most trusted counselor Ahithophel advised his leader to make a bold statement of his break with David. Ahithophel's advice was to take the ten concubines David left in Jerusalem onto the roof of the royal palace and publicly rape them. This Absalom did.

■ *As David fled from Jerusalem, he was met by*
■ *both supporters and detractors. Ziba aided*
■ *David, while Shimei cursed him. Absalom*
■ *entered Jerusalem, then followed Ahitho-*
■ *phel's advice to rape David's concubines*
■ *publicly.*

2 SAMUEL 17

DAVID ARRIVES IN MAHANAIM
(17:1–29)

Attempts to Kill David (vv. 1–14)

Ahithophel had a second piece of advice for
Absalom—have a relatively small force attack
David and his group immediately, while they
were disorganized and on the run, with the purpose of killing only David. Absalom liked
Ahithophel's advice but decided to consult
Hushai before acting on it. Hushai used this
opportunity to try to save David's life by presenting a grand but actually inept military strategy: Stay away from David's forces until a huge
army could be raised, then carry out a slow,
grinding campaign that would crush all David's
forces. Though Ahithophel's plan was better,
the Lord caused Absalom to prefer Hushai's.

A Warning for David (vv. 15–22)

Even so, Hushai was not confident that David
would be safe if he spent the night west of the
Jordan River. Consequently, he had Zadok and
Abiathar send their sons Ahimaaz and Jonathan
to David, warning him of the danger. Though
David and his group were exhausted from the

day's activities, they spent the entire night crossing the river.

Ahithophel's Death (vv. 23–26)

Ahithophel, realizing that Absalom's decision would mean defeat for Absalom and his followers, left Jerusalem and returned to his hometown. Once there, he set his affairs in order and hanged himself. Absalom, however, went to work raising an army to prepare for battle with David. He appointed his cousin Amasa as commander of his forces.

David's Support (vv. 27–29)

Ironically, by staying in Mahanaim David resided in the same city where Ish-Bosheth, the man against whom David fought for the right to rule Israel, had also lived.

By this time David's group arrived at Mahanaim. There they received much-needed provisions of food, utensils, and bedding from Shobi and Barzillai, wealthy sympathizers who lived in the area.

■ *Choosing between alternate strategies for*
■ *attacking his father, Absalom opted to try a*
■ *massive, slow-moving attack against David.*
■ *Absalom's foolish decision gave David time*
■ *to escape and organize his forces at Maha-*
■ *naim, east of the Jordan River.*

2 SAMUEL 18

ABSALOM DIES ON THE BATTLEFIELD (18:1–33)

Battle with Absalom (vv. 1–5)

Organizing his army at Mahanaim, David divided up command of the troops among three men, Joab, Abishai, and Ittai. David did not lead the troops himself into battle because his men considered the risk of losing him too great. Instead he remained at Mahanaim when his troops went into battle against Absalom's forces. Before the troops left, however, David ordered his commanders to spare Absalom's life.

Absalom's Death (vv. 6–18)

Facing the massive Israelite army, David's forces chose to fight in the forest of Ephraim, a battle site that favored the smaller army. While riding a mule under an oak in the forest, Absalom's head got caught in some branches. His mule ran away, leaving him dangling helplessly above the ground. David's troops discovered him in this condition and reported it to Joab, who then went out with a squadron of men, killed him, and buried his body under a large pile of rocks. When the Israelite army learned of their leader's death, they quit fighting and fled to their homes. Absalom died without leaving any male heir. Apparently his three sons died in childhood.

By rebelling against his father and having relations with members of his father's harem, Absalom had come under God's curse (see Deut. 27:16, 20). Fittingly, by dying on a tree he died the death of one under God's curse (see Deut. 21:23).

David's Grief (vv. 19–33)

In Mahanaim, David awaited word from messengers regarding the outcome of the battle and especially the fate of Absalom. When David learned of his son's death, he was overcome with emotion. Going up into his chamber above the gateway to the city, he burst into tears and cried out loudly. In his words he expressed the wish to have died in place of his son.

■ *Led by Joab, Abishai, and Ittai, David's*
■ *forces fought and defeated Absalom's army*
■ *in the forest of Ephraim. In the battle*
■ *Absalom was killed, an event that brought*
■ *profound grief to David.*

QUESTIONS TO GUIDE YOUR STUDY

1. What were some of the consequences of David's sin within his own family?
2. What were the consequences of Absalom's rebellion against his father?

2 SAMUEL 19

DAVID RETURNS FROM EXILE (19:1–43)

Congratulations for Victory (vv. 1–8a)
When Israel's troops learned that David was grieving deeply over the death of his son, their pride in victory turned into shame. David's chief commander, Joab, was incensed at the king's obvious lack of gratitude. After all, the troops had saved the lives of David and his family. Accordingly, he ordered David to congratulate the troops for their victory. This David did.

David's Return to Jerusalem (vv. 8b–15a)
The remnants of Absalom's army, meanwhile, fled to their homes. The Israelites who had supported Absalom in the revolt asked David to return to Jerusalem as their king. With the assistance of Amasa, David's designated replacement for Joab as chief commander, the leaders of the tribe of Judah also agreed to have David return as their king. When David was assured of being accepted by both the Israelites and the Juda-

hites, he led his group to cross the Jordan River and return to Jerusalem.

Special Favors (vv. 15b–40)

The king's group was met at the Jordan River by large numbers of people who had come to help them cross the river. Besides large armed delegations from Judah, Benjamin, and Israel, some individuals came seeking a special favor from the returning king. Among these were Shimei (see 16:5–13) and Mephibosheth. As a gesture of goodwill, David let Shimei live and gave back to Mephibosheth half of his grandfather's estate. Before crossing, David also rewarded Barzillai, a man who had provided food for David's group at Mahanaim, by letting Kimham—apparently Barzillai's son—become a permanent member of the royal court.

Evidence that David kept his promise to treat Kimham well is found in Jeremiah 41:17, where mention is made of a site near Bethlehem known as Geruth Kimham ("the hospitality of/ accorded to Kimham").

Depth of Mistrust (vv. 41–43)

The depth of mistrust that existed between the armies of Judah and Israel was seen when the Israelite army argued vehemently with the Judahites over the fact that more Judahites than Israelites got to help David cross the Jordan.

■ *At Joab's urging, David set aside his grief,*
■ *thanked his troops for their help, and then*
■ *began the journey back to Jerusalem. David*
■ *and his group were assisted in their return by*
■ *people from Judah and Israel. As he reen-*
■ *tered Israel, David granted special favors to*
■ *a friend as well as to former enemies.*

DAVID REENTERS JERUSALEM, THEN QUELLS SHEBA'S REBELLION (20:1–26)

David Rejected (vv. 1–2)

The heated argument that arose between the men from Judah and those of the rest of Israel took an ugly turn as Sheba the Benjamite, a relative of King Saul, rallied the non-Judahites to reject David as their king and leave.

David's Claim to the Throne (vv. 3–5)

As soon as David returned to Jerusalem, he took steps to reassert his claim of kingship over Israel. First he dealt with the issue of the ten concubines Absalom had raped. Their needs would be cared for properly, but they would have to live the rest of their lives as though they were widows. Then he dealt with Sheba's rebellion. David ordered Amasa, his new commander in chief, to mobilize Judah's army within three days, then go forth to do battle.

Joab as Commander (vv. 6–13)

When after three days Amasa still had not gotten Judah's army together, David ordered Abishai to lead David's royal brigade into battle against Sheba. Amasa and the troops of Judah met up with Abishai's forces as they were marching into Benjamite territory at Gibeon. There Joab, who was evidently jealous of the man who had replaced him as supreme commander of David's army, greeted Abishai and immediately murdered him. Then Joab took back control of David's army and began pursuing Sheba.

Attack at Abel Beth Maacah (vv. 14–23a)

The army of Judah caught up with Sheba at Abel Beth Maacah, some thirty miles north of the Sea of Galilee. An all-out attack was then launched against the walled city. The citizens of Abel panicked, and a wise woman spoke to Joab from the city wall asking what they could do to end the attack. Joab told her their city would be saved if they would hand over Sheba. Immediately the people of Abel arrested Sheba and beheaded him. Thus the rebellion was put down, and David's status as Israel's king was confirmed. For his efforts Joab was once again made the commander of Israel's armies.

Wise women played a role at several points in David's career. Besides the wise woman of Abel, other wise women included Abigail (see 1 Sam. 25) and the wise woman of Tekoa (see 2 Sam. 14). David's wife Michal also saved his life on one occasion by her prudent action (see 1 Sam. 19:11–14).

Administration of David's Reign (vv. 23b–26)

A list of administrators at the end of this chapter suggests that David's government remained relatively stable throughout his tenure as king. Toward the end of David's reign, he appears to have established a position for an administrator over forced laborers—that is, over conquered foreigners who were forced to perform labor in behalf of the Israelite nation. Also, his sons were no longer mentioned as being priests.

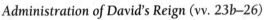

- David returned to Jerusalem and reasserted
- his control of the capital city and the nation.
- In the process he put down a second revolt,
- this one led by Sheba the Benjamite.

DAVID DEALS WITH THE GIBEONITES AND THE PHILISTINES (21:1–22)

Famine in the Land (vv. 1–9)

At some point in David's reign, a three-year-long famine plagued the land. David learned from the Lord that the famine was brought against Israel as a judgment for Saul's murderous treatment of the Gibeonites. Seeking to end the famine, David asked the Gibeonites what it would take to make amends with them. They said they wanted to kill seven of Saul's male descendants. David gave them permission to do this but insisted that Jonathan's son Mephibosheth be spared. Two sons of Saul by his concubine Rizpah and five of Saul's grandsons were killed by Gibeonites in the fall during a religious ceremony.

Rizpah's Devotion (vv. 10–14)

The bodies were left unburied but were spared from being ravaged by wild animals through the heroic efforts of Rizpah, who camped out next to the corpses for two months and drove away would-be attacking animals. When David learned of Rizpah's remarkable devotion to her departed relatives, he gathered together the bones of all the royal family, including those of Saul and Jonathan, and provided them with an honorable burial in the family tomb of Saul's father Kish in Zela. Following that, the famine ended in Israel.

Dangerous Encounters (vv. 15–22)

Over the years David and his soldiers had many dangerous encounters with the Philistines. Once when David was nearly exhausted, he was

According to 2 Samuel 21:19, Elhanan killed Goliath. However, this seems to contradict 1 Samuel 17, where David is said to have killed Goliath. In 1 Chronicles 20:5, Elhanan is said to have killed Goliath's brother, not Goliath himself. Apparently 2 Samuel 21:19 is an example of an ancient copyist's error—a problem in the text accidentally created by a person's making a handwritten copy of 2 Samuel from an old manuscript sometime before the time of Christ. Other suggestions include the possibility that Elhanan was another name for David, that Goliath was a title and not a name, and that there were two Goliaths of Gath.

forced to fight a giant named Ishbi-Benob. The king escaped death only because Abishai rescued him. Other formidable Philistines killed by Israelites include Saph, Goliath's brother, and an unnamed fighter who had twelve fingers and twelve toes.

■ *To end a three-year famine brought as judg-*
■ *ment against Israel, David permitted the*
■ *Gibeonites to avenge the family of Saul for*
■ *murders Saul had committed. Seven mem-*
■ *bers of Saul's family were executed. During*
■ *David's reign his soldiers killed four fear-*
■ *some Philistine heroes.*

2 SAMUEL 22

DAVID PRAISES GOD FOR HIS HELP (22:1–51)

David experienced God's saving help on many occasions throughout his lifetime. The king freely confessed that the Lord was the source of his success and expressed gratitude for the protection and success God provided to him. The lengthy poem found in this chapter—the longest quote in the Bible attributed to David—is essentially a restatement of Psalm 18, the longest psalm attributed to David. In its present setting it is used to reveal the religious core of Israel's most beloved and respected king.

Praise (vv. 1–4)

Here David expressed praise for the Lord. He compared God to a rock, a fortress, a stronghold, a refuge, and a shield.

Many parallels exist between 22:1–51 and Psalm 18. They appear to be the same basic poem, though their purposes are different. The usage in Samuel is intended to reveal the religious core of the primary narrative character in 1, 2 Samuel; Psalm 18 was intended for use as an aid in public worship.

God's Deliverance (vv. 5–20)

In this section David poetically recounted ways in which the Lord delivered David from various perils.

God's Law (vv. 21–29)

The theological center of the poem is found here, as David revealed the reason for his deliverance. It is because David was careful to follow the Law of the Lord.

Provision for Victory (vv. 30–46)

These verses provide further poetic descriptions of the Lord's deliverance of David from dangers. God's help enabled David to crush his enemies.

Praise for God's Power (vv. 47–50)

This section provides further words of praise for the Lord, recognizing that it was God who put conquered nations under David.

God's Unfailing Love (v. 51)

In the concluding verse of this poem, David suggested that God will show unfailing love to his family line forever.

■ *In the longest quote attributed to David in the*
■ *Bible, Israel's greatest king praised God for his*
■ *success and confessed that obedience to God's*
■ *Law was the reason for God's blessings on him.*

DAVID GIVES HIS FINAL ORACLE (23:1–7)

David the Prophet (vv. 1–5)

In this section David, who had previously been shown acting as a king and priest, now is shown in his role as a prophet. Here he presented the ideal of a righteous king who is guided by the fear of the Lord. This ideal king is poetically described by David as one who rules over his subjects in righteousness and through his policies brings enlightenment and vitality to his nation, much as the light of morning at sunrise brings brightness and life to a landscape.

The Righteous King (v. 6)

Besides bringing light and life to his nation, the righteous king depicted by David in this section also does battle with the godless and wicked. Such individuals are like thorns, whose destiny is to be burned so that their seeds will not grow and multiply in the land.

David's Confession (v. 7)

David confessed that God chose him and his descendants to be Israel's just and righteous kings. This happened when the Lord made an everlasting covenant with David. Christians understand Jesus Christ to be the ultimate example of a descendant of David who is a just and righteous king.

Early Jewish interpreters understood 23:1–7 to be a messianic passage. Many Christian interpreters have understood Jesus Christ to be the "light" spoken of in verse 4.

■ *Speaking as a prophet, David described the*
■ *ideal king over God's people. Such a man*
■ *fears God and is righteous and just. With*
■ *wonder David confessed that God had chosen*
■ *his family line to lead Israel.*

DAVID'S ARMY HAD VALIANT SOLDIERS (23:8–39)

Military Leaders (vv. 8–12)

David's great success in battle was not the result of just his own military skill and faith in God. It was also due to the efforts of the dedicated and talented soldiers under his command. In this section the most heroic of David's soldiers are listed along with seven of their most dramatic military achievements.

David established special ranks for his best soldiers. The most honored of David's soldiers were placed in a group known as The Three. Josheb-Basshebeth, Eleazar, and Shammah were in this category. Josheb-Basshebeth was made chief of this group when he personally killed eight hundred men in one battle.

Mutual Respect (vv. 13–17)

The most celebrated exploit of The Three appears to have taken place early in David's reign, when he was at the cave of Adullam and the Philistines were in the Valley of Rephaim (see 2 Sam. 5:17). In the cave David became thirsty and expressed the desire to drink water from the well of Bethlehem, his hometown. The Three made a secret journey to Bethlehem, sneaking through enemy lines to get water for David. When they gave it to David, he was so moved by their brave and thoughtful actions that he gave it as a special offering to the Lord without drinking any of it. This event showed both the bravery of David's men and David's respect for his men.

Acts of Bravery (vv. 18–23)

Abishai, David's nephew, was the commander of The Three. Benaiah, a Levite, who was commander of the Kerethites and Pelethites, performed many brave actions, including killing a lion in a hand-to-hand struggle.

The Thirty (vv. 24–39)

The second most-honored group in David's army was The Thirty. Among the fighters included in this group were Elhanan, who killed Goliath's brother, and Uriah, Bathsheba's husband.

Throughout the course of David's reign, a total of thirty-seven men were admitted to the ranks of The Thirty.

Lions were once feared predators in Israel (see Judg. 14:5–6; 1 Sam. 17:34; 1 Kings 13:24). They are now extinct in Israel, the last one being killed there in the thirteenth century A.D.

■ *David honored his most valiant soldiers by*
■ *giving them special ranks. David's best sol-*
■ *diers became members of The Three. Others*
■ *were admitted to the ranks of The Thirty.*
■ *These men performed many heroic acts in*
■ *Israel's behalf.*

The Torah indicated that a plague would result from a military census that was carried out improperly (see Exod. 30:12).

2 SAMUEL 24

DAVID STOPS A PLAGUE RESULTING FROM A SINFUL CENSUS (24:1–25)

Improper Census (vv. 1–2)
Sometime after David had conquered Jerusalem, God became angry with Israel and incited David to take an improper census of his soldiers. Exactly what was wrong about the census is not stated, but it could be either David's motivation or the fact that he carried it out in a way that violated the Torah guidelines (see Exod. 30:12–13).

Joab's Protests (vv. 3–9)
Despite the protests of Joab, David ordered his highest officers to go throughout Israelite territory and count all the men eligible for military service. Accordingly, Joab led the men in a nine-and-a-half-month journey through Israelite lands both east and west of the Jordan River. A total of 1.3 million men were counted, half a million of which were from Judah.

Three-Day Plague (vv. 10–14)
Because there was something wrong with the census, God announced through the prophet Gad that Israel would be judged. However, David could choose between three possible punishments—a three-year famine, three months of military defeats, or a three-day plague. David chose the plague, believing that since God (and not a human) would have to carry it out, He might mercifully spare Israel.

Sacrifices to God (vv. 15–25)
Seventy thousand people died in the plague; but when the death angel came to the outskirts of Jerusalem, God ordered it to stop. The prophet

Gad told David to offer up sacrifices at the threshing floor of Araunah, the spot where the angel stopped. David not only did that, but he also bought Araunah's threshing floor, oxen, and wooden plows—the latter two purchases being used as sacrificial animals and fuel for the altar fire. Later this spot would become the site of the Temple of the Lord.

■ *To punish Israel for sin, God caused David to*
■ *order an improper census, a deed which led*
■ *to a plague in which seventy thousand Isra-*
■ *elites died. The plague was stopped when*
■ *David purchased Araunah's threshing floor*
■ *and offered sacrifices to God there.*

QUESTIONS TO GUIDE YOUR STUDY

1. Read David's poem in 2 Samuel 22. What are some of the characteristics of God expressed in this poem?
2. Read David's description of a just ruler in 2 Samuel 23:2–4? To what does David liken a just ruler?

REFERENCE SOURCES USED

The following is a collection of Broadman & Holman published reference sources used for this work. They are provided here to meet the reader's need for more specific information and/or an expanded treatment of 1 and 2 Samuel. All of these works will greatly aid in the reader's study, teaching, and presentation of 1, 2 Samuel. The accompanying annotations can be helpful in guiding the reader to the proper resources.

Bergen, Robert, The New American Commentary, vol. 7, *1, 2 Samuel*. A theological commentary on 1 &2 Samuel.

Cate, Robert L. *An Introduction to the Historical Books of the Old Testament*. A survey of the books of Joshua through Esther with special attention to issues of history writing in ancient Israel.

Cate, Robert L. *An Introduction to the Old Testament and Its Study*. An introductory work presenting background information, issues related to interpretation, and summaries of each book of the Old Testament.

Dockery, David S., Kenneth A. Mathews, and Robert B. Sloan. *Foundations for Biblical Interpretation: A Complete Library of Tools and Resources*. A comprehensive introduction to matters relating to the composition and interpretation of the entire Bible. This work includes a discussion of the geographical, historical, cultural, religious, and political backgrounds of the Bible.

Francisco, Clyde T. *Introducing the Old Testament*. Revised edition. An introductory guide to each of the books of the Old Testament. This work includes a discussion on how to interpret the Old Testament.

Holman Bible Dictionary. An exhaustive, alphabetically arranged resource of Bible-related subjects. An excellent tool of definitions and other information on the people, places, things, and events of the Bible.

Holman Bible Handbook. A summary treatment of each book of the Bible that offers outlines, commentary on key themes and sections, illustrations, charts, maps, and full-color photos. This tool also provides an accent on broader theological teachings of the Bible.

Holman Book of Biblical Charts, Maps, and Reconstructions. This easy-to-use work provides numerous color charts on various matters related to Bible content and background, maps of important events, and drawings of objects, buildings, and cities mentioned in the Bible.

Lewis, Joe O. Layman's Bible Book Commentary, vol. 5, *1 & 2 Samuel, 1 Chronicles*. A concise commentary on 1, 2 Samuel.

Sandy, D. Brent, and Ronald L. Giese Jr. *Cracking Old Testament Codes: A Guide to Interpreting the Literary Genres of the Old Testament*. This book is designed to make scholarly discussions available to preachers and teachers.

Smith, Ralph L. *Old Testament Theology: Its History, Method, and Message*. A comprehensive treatment of various issues relating to Old Testament theology. Written for university and seminary students, ministers, and advanced lay teachers.

SHEPHERD'S NOTES

_____

_____

_____

_____

_____

_____

_____

_____

_____

_____

_____

_____

_____

_____

_____

_____

_____

_____

_____

_____

_____

_____

SHEPHERD'S NOTES

SHEPHERD'S
NOTES